TWO FAT LADIES
FULL THROTTLE

TWO FAT LADIES
FULL THROTTLE

Jennifer Paterson and
Clarissa Dickson Wright

First published in 1998

Text © Optomen Television and
Jennifer Paterson and Clarissa Dickson
Wright 1998
Photographs © Ebury Press or
Optomen Television 1998

Jennifer Paterson and Clarissa Dickson
Wright have asserted their right to be
identified as the authors of this work
under the Copyright, Designs and
Patents Act 1988.

Published in Canada in 1998 by
élan press, an imprint of
General Publishing Co. Limited
30 Lesmill Road
Toronto, Canada M3B 2T6

First published in the United Kingdom
in 1998 by Ebury Press
Random House, 20 Vauxhall Bridge
Road, London SW1V 2SA

Canadian Cataloguing in Publication
Data is available from the National
Library of Canada

ISBN 1-55144-199-3

Designed by Alison Shackleton
Food photography by James Murphy
Food styling by Alison Birch
Styling by Róisín Nield

Printed and bound in the UK by Butler
and Tanner Ltd, Frome, Somerset

Acknowledgements

To Pat Llewellyn, our own beloved Dr Frankenstein, who we really,
really love and adore! (She made us say the last bit.)

Peter Gillbe, tireless in his efforts. We've never seen jet-lag worn so
lightly and Diogenes could die happy.

Lesley – the blessed return of Lesley has saved all our sanities.

Darling Spike, our cameraman/director, who has brought a whole
new toy box to our nursery.

Bridget, our co-ordinator, without whom nothing would ever move
and who could do the equestrian stunts to boot.

Polly, beloved researcher, known as 'Polly who is not going to put the
kettle on any more.' Our beautiful lioness is leaving us for higher things.

Guy (de Montfort), our new little bambi (6'3"), a welcome, angelic
addition and not just a pretty face but a great researcher too.

Corinne, a paragon of efficiency and, as Jennifer said, when she says
'Talk to you later' you know, unfortunately, that she means it!

(Saint) Luke, our other cameraman, still the finest croquet player on
the team.

Sara, our valiant camera operator, who risked life and limb with bees
and oarsmen alike.

Louis, naughty little Louis, 'lucky 21-year-old toy boy', the billiardo king.

Billy, our beloved team heart-throb.

Rex, dearly beloved, who would be totally perfect if he would only
eat meat.

Our editor, Paul Ratcliffe, a tireless perfectionist who makes sure our
mistakes remain on the cutting room floor.

Ginny, a madonna, even in her apron, and with the temperament
to boot.

Elaine – how can one work so hard on a diet of mini-cheddars
and doughnuts?

Dear Basil Comely, genius as ever, and proud father of the book title,
Full Throttle.

Mark Thompson, 'darling Ignatius', thank God for a Papist controller.

Thanks to Adam Kemp and Jane Root, our stalwart supporters at the BBC.

And thanks to Fiona MacIntyre, Penny Simpson and Isabel Duffy, the
still long-suffering gang at Ebury Press.

CONTENTS

INTRODUCTION

Outside Paddy Coyne's pub in Ireland, with the publican and

lobster fishermen

It wasn't until halfway through my conversation with Clarissa that I realised my exciting news was going down like a soufflé in a draught.

'America?' she barked down the 'phone. 'You don't really expect me to go to America?' I should have known. After vegetarians and super-markets, Clarissa holds the home of the hamburger responsible for everything that's wrong with the modern world – including fast food, political correctness and plastic surgery. But for British television producers, the merest whiff of American interest causes ripples of excitement and inspires the construction of lav-ish castles in the air. So if you're offered a promotional tour by a broadcaster you only hes-

itate long enough to throw some clothes into a bag and run to the airport. Clarissa, however, was determined to stick to her principles.

I was confident of Jennifer though. I knew she'd want to go. She'd lived in the States for a while and had rather enjoyed it. She's also a big fan of old American films.

'I would like to see Hollywood,' she said, 'but isn't Los Angeles rather hot? You know I can't stand the heat and think of my poor feet.' (Jennifer had spent the last month with each toe wrapped in banana skin to cure her warts.) Desperate measures were called for. 'But Clarissa's dying to go,' I explained, silently offer-ing up a prayer for absolution.

'Jennifer's dying to go,' I explained to Clarissa. 'She says she has to see Hollywood before she dies.' I made a mental note that my earlier prayer should hold good for two lies rather than just the one.

'Americans are intrigued by good manners, in part because they don't have any.' We were on the aeroplane going to America. Clarissa was on my right, reading aloud from *The Xenophobe's Guide To The Americans*. On my left sat Jennifer, whose dreams of Hollywood had taken a battering. She'd just seen *Jurassic Park* and was very confused. 'Who was that fat man in the laboratory? Do you know?' she asked me. She sought assistance from the air hostess. 'Have you seen Jurassic Park? Did you understand what that fat man was stealing?' That neither of us could tell her confirmed that Hollywood was a very different place from the days of Norma Desmond when it was only the sun that went down on Sunset Boulevard. 'Why don't they make films like they used to?' Jennifer wanted to know. We were at 30,000ft but I could still feel my heart sinking. Even a fistful of dollars wasn't going to make this trip worthwhile.

When we arrived in New York there were several huge limousines lined up outside the terminal. 'Ugh, Americans have to do everything bigger than everyone else.' Clarissa grumped. 'So ostentatious and vulgar,' Jennifer agreed. At this, the driver of the biggest limousine, less a car and more of a sitting room on wheels, got out

with a board with the Ladies' names on. 'I suppose we'll just have to put up with it,' said Clarissa, disappearing inside. Seconds later Jennifer's voice boomed out of the darkness. 'My dear, there's a bar in here.' I breathed an American-sized sigh of relief – things were looking up.

The whole of the USA seemed to have developed Fatladymania – everywhere they went people were genuinely delighted to see them. Live chat shows, book signings, interviews for newspapers and magazines were all crammed into our rather breathless timetable. At our book signing in New York, people were queuing round the block. Some had brought presents. One woman had learned the programme credits off by heart – she reeled off the names of everyone on the production team and wanted to know all about them. 'What does Luke Cardiff look like? And Polly Livingston? Is she married?'

We were whisked to Los Angeles to stay at the palatial Chateau Marmont. My suite was so enormous that I got lost on the way to the bedroom. We were sitting in the bar before dinner one evening when I became rather excited – Keanu Reeves was sitting at the other side of the room. 'Oh for goodness sake Patricia you're so star struck,' Jennifer said. 'Who on earth is Keanu Reeves?' Clarissa wanted to know, so I pointed him out as discreetly as I could. 'Oh him,' she said, waving enthusiastically. 'He's the nice young man I've been chatting with beside the

Jennifer and Clarissa trip the light fantastic at Kylemore Abbey in Co. Galway

pool all afternoon. He never mentioned he was an actor. In fact, we talked about vegetables.'

On our last evening in New York, we went to a wonderful Japanese restaurant called Nobu. We were treated like queens by the maitre d' who was clearly besotted. He kept ordering delicious morsels for us from the kitchen and introducing us proudly to his regular diners. One gentleman we met worked for Steven Spielberg, the director of *Jurassic Park*. Jennifer leapt in without pausing for breath. 'Oh good. Who was that fat man in the laboratory? Do you know?

What was he stealing?' He seemed a little taken aback, but after ten minutes all was clear.

For a programme that most people thought would not get many viewers outside the Home Counties, it's been a bumper year. The series has sold all over the world (it's great with Hebrew subtitles but even better dubbed into Japanese) and the Ladies seem to be more in demand than ever. They even got invited to one of the Prime Minister and Mrs Blair's famous media parties at Downing Street. Clarissa didn' t want to go as she's still fuming about the beef on the bone ban, so I got to be Cinderella. We had a delightful evening, marred only by the fact that Jennifer wasn't allowed to smoke. For some reason, every news programme that needs footage to cover a story about Labour Party sleaze uses footage of Jennifer meeting Mrs Blair. I fail to see what's so sleazy about an elderly Catholic lady who's a spinster of the parish of Westminster swapping recipes with one of the country's leading QCs (although if the government brings in a tax cut on motorbikes with sidecars, they'd have every right to be suspicious).

This book accompanies our third television series. We've had another summer travelling around the country to weird and wonderful locations, praying for sunny weather. Who knows where we'll be next, but we hope that you will be watching.

Pat Llewellyn
Series Producer

SOUPS AND STARTERS

This is the life! Jennifer and Clarissa go punting in Cambridge

Our TV programme is about menus this year and I would like you to keep the thought of the menu with you at all times whilst reading this book.

The first course is many people's favourite part of the meal, indeed there was once a highly successful London restaurant that served nothing but starters and puddings. In many ways, the first course is like a TV trail or an advertisement: you want to grab the attention of your guests away from their drinks and their pre-dinner chat and refocus them on to the fact that they are now sitting down to enjoy your food. If you don't do this you will feel like the chef in the Saki story who ran amok and drowned the bandleader in the soup tureen because everyone was listening to the music and ignoring his efforts!

Carry the concept of your whole menu with you at all times. If your main course is light, then you can afford a more robust starter. When we were cooking for the Cambridge University Rowing Eight the main course was a fairly light rabbit dish of mine with a sort of hot salad in the form of Jennifer's Peas with Lettuce and so, knowing how hungry they would be, as a starter we gave them a substantial bean soup full of Spanish sausages, ham hocks and other good things (for less hearty appetites this would make a very good main course). The capacity of your guests is another thing to be considered - those

Clarissa goes digital during a tea break

I like my starters to have a punch and because nowadays many ingredients are so flavourless that you have to work round them rather than with them, the salmon mousse I served to the lawyers of Lincoln's Inn had blue cheese in it, they loved it but I would not spoil good wild salmon by using that recipe.

Above all don't lose sight of your menu, focus on the perspective of the meal when choosing your starter and remember the colours of the meal – nothing is worse than an all white menu, and the different courses should appeal to the eye as well as the stomach.

glorious golden young men will grow into dilettantes whose ravished palates and sensitive digestions need both titillating and nurturing. Incindentally the oarsmen were so fit that when we were trying to keep pace with them on the tow path the bike could barely keep up! It gives a whole different picture to the historic use of water transport to imagine Henry VIII's great gilded barge powered by the likes of those young giants. So much nicer than our dear present Queen's gas-powered taxi!

Some of the best starters are of course the simplest. As I write we are just entering the asparagus season, and nothing can be nicer than well-cooked new season asparagus with melted butter or hollandaise. However, as Jennifer pointed out in last year's Christmas special, we don't get paid to tell you to serve a plate of smoked salmon. In cold weather soups are good value, but be careful with cold summer soups – in Scotland, for instance, many people don't seem to like them much and many men think they are a mere frivolity.

Jennifer enjoys filming in another great British summer

Cosmopolitan

This is not strictly a starter, it is a cocktail, but certainly something to start a meal with a bang. I was given the recipe by Alan Kearney, the well-known New York barman, on a recent trip to New York. He made one for Patricia, our beloved director, upon whom they seemed to have a very strange effect. She took to dancing with strangers in the hotel bar and refused to go to bed, very unlike her. Delicious – but proceed with caution.

EACH DRINK SHOULD BE MADE OF:

80 parts lemon vodka
10 parts Cointreau
8 parts cranberry juice
2 parts lime juice

Shake and strain. Lethal!

JP

Baden Leek Soup

This recipe comes from Baden Baden the well-known German health spa and it is a nourishing comforting soup. The 'honest toun' of Musselburgh where I live is famous for its leeks, even the ancient Romans praised and exported Musselburgh leeks. It was only in this century that the species was registered and named by the great botanist and horticulturist, Mr Scarlett. It is a soup I often make with our excellent leeks.

4 leeks
55g/2oz butter
2 onions, finely chopped
1.75 litres/3 pints good chicken stock
salt and freshly ground pepper
300ml/½ pint milk
1 medium potato, cooked and mashed
115g/4oz good ham, chopped
120ml/4fl oz cream
finely chopped parsley, to serve

Trim and wash the leeks leaving some of the green. Slice thinly. Melt the butter in a large pan and sauté the leeks and onions until soft. Add stock and seasoning, bring to the boil and simmer for 15 minutes.Mix the milk and mashed potato together and stir into the sauce, return to the boil and allow to thicken. Remove from the heat and stir in the ham and cream, return to the heat but do not allow to boil. Serve sprinkled with parsley.

CDW

Beetroot Soup

This is not a real Russian beetroot soup, but a wonderful colour nevertheless. It is quite filling and suitable as a supper dish with very little to follow, or you might like it chilled having removed any fat that rises to the top.

900ml/1½ pints chicken stock
225g/8 oz beetroot, chopped and cleaned
225g/8 oz potatoes, chopped and cleaned
115g/4oz carrots, chopped
115g/4oz parsnips, chopped
55g/2oz celery, fibres removed
I leek, finely sliced
1 large onion, chopped
1 clove of garlic, finely chopped
55g/2oz goose or chicken fat, or 1 tbsp vegetable oil
1 tsp mixed herbs (*herbes Provençal*)
25g/1oz butter
1 tbsp finely chopped parsley

OPTIONAL:
tomato purée
orange juice
red wine
sherry
soured cream

Bring stock to the boil, add beetroot, potatoes, carrots, parsnips, celery, green leek tops and simmer for about 1 hour. (Beetroot takes a long time to cook!) In the meantime, fry the onions, white part of leek and garlic in the fat or oil in a frying pan until the onions begin to brown, stirring continuously, add the herbs and fry a little longer. Add these ingredients to the saucepan and just bring to the boil. Allow to cool for 5 minutes and add the chopped parsley and then liquidise.

You may enhance the colour of the soup by adding tomato purée – and give flavour by adding either orange juice, red wine or sherry. A swirl of soured cream may be added when serving.

JP

Asturian Bean and Sausage Soup

My mad wild friends the Herbie boys from the delicatessen of that name in Edinburgh gave me a *mercillo* or Spanish blood sausage, and in return I gave them this recipe. Do not confuse Asturia, which is a Spanish Kingdom, with the land of *lederhosen*. This is a good rib-sticking soup and a meal in itself.

250g/9oz white beans, soaked overnight
200g/7oz ham hock, soaked for 1 hour
140g/5oz belly of pork rib, on the bone
140g/5oz belly of pork, cubed
3 fresh *mercillos* or other or blood pudding
2 or 3 *chorizo* sausages
750g/1½lb dark green cabbage
450g/1lb potatoes
salt and freshly ground black pepper
pinch of paprika, optional

Put all the ingredients except the cabbage and potatoes into a pan and cover with water. Skim as the water comes to the boil and cook for 1 hour or until the beans are almost tender. Cut up the cabbage quite finely and bring to the boil in a saucepan of salted water. Drain. Remove the meat bones returning any shreds of meat to the casserole and slice the sausages. Season with plenty of black pepper and salt to taste. Add the cabbage and potatoes, and more liquid if necessary to cover them comfortably. Simmer until the potatoes are tender and check the seasoning. If your *chorizos* are not very spicy, you could add some paprika. Serve in big bowls with country bread.

CDW

Fish Soup

This is a simple soup, very suitable for the days in Lent. It has a good flavour and a sufficient feel of penitence about it to please the most rigid of worshippers.

1 large cod's head
1 large onion
1 clove of garlic, chopped
1 stick celery, chopped
1 carrot, chopped
1 tomato, skinned and chopped
1 tbsp olive oil
25g/1oz butter
pinch each of thyme, sage, dill and saffron
1 bayleaf
900ml/1½ pints water
1 tbsp tomato purée
1 tbsp rice
salt and freshly ground pepper
croûtons, to serve

Fry onion, garlic, chopped stick of celery, chopped carrot and tomato in olive oil and butter until the onions are opaque, add the herbs and fry for a little longer. Add the cod's head and bayleaf and water. Bring to the boil and then simmer for about 1 hour. Strain into another saucepan, add the tomato purée and rice and boil for 10 minutes. Add salt and pepper to taste. Fry some croûtons in olive oil and serve with the soup.

JP

Chicken and Ginger Soup

It is difficult to find a proper boiling fowl these days. The best places to look are Chinese shops, where they are called endearingly 'old hen', or Halal butchers. It seems to me that our ethnic communities have priorities we would be well encouraged to emulate. In my recent visit to Smithfield Market for filming, I was interested to notice the large number of Chinese and West Indians who were painstakingly choosing such vital items as pigs' trotters and heads or old hens. This is an Asian-style soup and tastes nicely of ginger.

1 boiling fowl (old hen)
1.75 litres/3 pints water
1 tbsp oil
1 onion, finely sliced
1 tbsp finely shredded ginger
750g/1½lb shredded Chinese leaves or spinach
soy sauce
2 eggs, beaten

Cut the chicken into pieces and boil for 1 hour in salted water. Strain retaining the stock, remove skin and bones from chicken and shred the flesh. If the stock has not enough flavour return the bones to it and boil to reduce, then restrain. Heat the oil in a pan and cook the onion gently until soft, add ginger and fry for 1 minute. Strain the chicken stock into this mixture, add the shredded chicken and cabbage. Simmer gently for 10 minutes, beat eggs and pour into soup stirring as you pour. Serve at once.

CDW

Green Rice Soup

This delicious and unusual soup comes from Sri Owen's brilliant *Rice Book.* The sorrel gives it a tart refreshing taste, and as it is an anti-scorbutic is a better way of imbibing vitamin C than chewing tablets. If you have no sorrel use spinach or chard. Make sure you use a good rich stock and fresh grated nutmeg.

2 tbsp olive oil or butter
3 shallots or 1 onion, chopped
1 clove of garlic, chopped
¼ tsp grated nutmeg
pinch of salt
¼ tsp white pepper
1.2 litres/2 pints stock
85g/3oz cooked white rice
150g/6oz sorrel, spinach or chard

In a large saucepan heat the oil or butter and sweat the shallots, or onion, and garlic. Add the nutmeg, salt and pepper and pour on the stock. I use chicken stock but a good flavoured vegetable stock, or pork or veal, will do as well. Bring to the boil and add the rice. Simmer for 10 minutes and add the sorrel or other greens, simmer for a further 4 minutes. Transfer to a liquidiser and process till smooth, if too thick add a little more stock, cook for a few minutes longer, stirring frequently. Serve hot or cold.

CDW

Garbure

This is a French cabbage soup, not unlike the Italian minestrone but without the pasta. A good hearty meal in itself. The goose fat gives an inimitable flavour and can be bought in cans in good grocery stores or delicatessens.

450g/1lb piece of gammon
1.2 litres/2 pints water
1 large potato
1 small swede
1 carrot
1 bouquet garni
1 bayleaf
350g/12oz spring cabbage, shredded
1 large onion, finely chopped
2 cloves of garlic, finely chopped
55g/2oz goose fat or 1 tbsp each of vegetable oil and butter
1 tbsp chopped parsley
pinch of thyme
salt and freshly ground pepper
croûtons, to serve

Put the gammon in a pan, add the water and bring to the boil. Reduce the heat and simmer until the gammon is cooked. Remove gammon and set aside. In the meantime peel the potato, swede and carrot and chop into smallish chunks. Cook these root vegetables in the stock and add the bouquet garni and the bayleaf. Wash the cabbage and shred. Gently fry the onion and garlic in the goose fat, add the pinch of thyme and stir in the onions.

The root vegetables should now be cooked, add the fried onions and garlic to them and then liquidise. Put this soup back in the saucepan, bring to the boil and add the shredded cabbage and cook for a further 10 minutes. Add the chopped parsley. Fry the croûtons in some more of the goose fat or oil and butter. Cut the pieces of gammon into small chunks, place in serving bowls and ladle the soup over. Serve with croûtons.

JP

19

Potage Billy By

This recipe was invented for the sole purpose of pandering to American snobbishness about eating mussels with their fingers. A very good customer by the name of William Brand of Ciro's in Deauville having invited some American friends to lunch asked the chef, Pierre Franey, to concoct a soup which included the juices of the mussels but not the mussels themselves. It was such a success it became established as Potage Billy Brand. Discretion, eventually, changed the name to Potage Billy By or sometimes Billy Bi.

900g/2lb mussels
1 tbsp porridge oats
4 shallots, chopped
55g/2oz butter
300ml/½ pint dry white wine
1 bouquet garni
1 bayleaf
6 peppercorns
1.2 litres/2 pints fish stock
600ml/1 pint whipping cream
2 egg yolks
1 tbsp chopped parsley
salt and freshly ground pepper

Wash and scrape the mussels, making sure the beard is removed. Leave for a couple of hours or overnight in salted water to which you have added the porridge oats. In a large saucepan fry the shallots and celery in the butter for about 3 minutes before adding the dry white wine, bouquet garni, bayleaf, peppercorns and mussels. Cook over a high heat, with the lid on, shaking the saucepan very often until the mussels open. This should take about 10 minutes. Remove all the mussels and strain the residual liquid through a muslin sieve. Add the fish stock and bring to the boil and allow to simmer for about 30 minutes. Allow to cool, then add the cream and heat up once again, bringing just to the boil, stirring continuously. Cool for 2 minutes. Ladle a little liquid into the egg yolks and whisk, and then add this to the soup with the chopped parsley, stirring well. Add salt and pepper if need be.

JP

Brazil Nut Soup

When I was six my father took my mother and me to Brazil. We stayed there for several months as he wanted to learn about snake venom. I remember that when I came home the nuns asked me what I had liked best and I said *Fejoiada*. It was, I think, the place where I first realised that different countries had different food. This is a strange soup and to me very reminiscent of the country.

350g/12oz brazil nuts
1.75 litres/3 pints good chicken stock
55g/2oz unsalted butter
55g/2oz plain flour
salt and freshly ground pepper
¼ tsp ground mace
250ml/8fl oz double cream
2 pomegranates

Heat the oven to 200°C/400°F/Gas 6. Toast the nuts for 10 minutes turning occasionally. Cool and rub the skins off the nuts. Grind finely in a food processor. Heat stock in a large pan, add a ladle of stock to the food processor and pulse until smooth. In a saucepan melt the butter and stir in the flour. Add the stock a little at a time and season with salt, pepper, mace and cream. Simmer gently for 20 minutes. If the soup is too thick stir in more cream. Strain the juice of one pomegranate into the soup. Serve the soup in warm plates, and top with seeds from the remaining pomegranate.

CDW

Welsh Rarebit Soufflés

I think nearly everybody enjoys cheese dishes. This is a variation on the original Welsh rarebit which was in fact pure toasted cheese cooked in the oven. It makes a very good supper dish, or when cut into small pieces, an excellent morsel to go with drinks.

225g/8oz really good mature Cheddar cheese, grated
4 eggs, separated
dry English mustard
Worcestershire sauce
Tabasco
salt and freshly ground pepper
2 large slices of good white bread

Place the cheese in a bowl, beat in 3 egg yolks (use the fourth one in something else), a level teaspoon of mustard, a good shake of Worcestershire sauce and Tabasco, and season to taste. Toast the bread. Whip the 4 egg whites until they stand in stiff peaks. Add a spoonful or so to the cheese mixture then gently fold the rest of them into the bowl. Put the toasts into an ovenproof dish and pour the mixture over them. Bake in a preheated oven at 230°C/450°F/Gas 8 for 10 minutes until browned and risen. Serve at once with a salad or spinach on the side.

JP

Red Peppers Stuffed with Aubergine Purée

Aubergine, eggplant and melanzane are all the same vegetable in different languages, and a favourite of mine. It can be used in so many ways, from delicious fritters to poor man's caviar. These red peppers stuffed with purée give you a double whammy and really are the full monty.

3 medium-sized aubergines
3 tbsp olive oil
1 large clove of garlic, finely chopped
juice of a large lemon
3 tbsp chopped parsley
salt and freshly ground black pepper
4 large red peppers

Make the aubergine purée by grilling the aubergines until the skins are charred and starting to blister which should mean that the pulp inside is soft. Leave to cool slightly then remove the skin by rubbing gently under cold water. Liquidise with the olive oil and then blend in the garlic, lemon juice, 2 tablespoons parsley, salt and pepper. Pour the purée into a bowl.

Cut the peppers in half, remove the stalk and seeds, brush the inside with the remaining olive oil and bake in a moderate oven 180°C/350°F/Gas 4 for about 30 minutes. A quarter of an hour before serving, fill the pepper halves with the aubergine purée, replace in the oven to warm through. After 15 minutes remove the peppers from the oven, sprinkle with remaining parsley and serve with plain toasted bread fingers.

JP

Mushroom Pasties

This is a medieval recipe from Maggie Black's excellent *The Medieval Cookbook* which she produced for the British Museum Press. I first served these patties at a lunch which I did for dear Michael Bateman and the *Independent on Sunday* where they had great acclaim. They are excellent for drinks parties or a buffet.

FOR THE PASTRY:
280g/10oz plain flour
½ tsp salt
85g/3oz butter
85g/3oz lard

FOR THE FILLING:
450g/1lb mushrooms (Paris mushrooms are best)
2 tbsp olive oil
salt and freshly ground black pepper
55g/2oz Cheddar cheese, grated
¼ tsp dry mustard
1 egg, beaten

To make the pastry cases, sift the flour into a bowl and rub in the butter and lard. Press into a dough, adding a little iced water if necessary to bind.

With two thirds of the pastry line small deep patty-pans. Chill. Preheat oven to 200°C/400°F/Gas 6. Trim off mushroom stalks, put the tops into a sieve and dip the mushrooms into boiling water. Drain them then pat dry and chop. Put them into a bowl and mix in the oil, cheese and seasonings. Fill the pastry cases with the mixture. Roll out the remaining pastry and make lids for the cases. Seal the lids with the beaten egg. Make a small x-cut in the centre of each lid. Bake in the oven for 15–18 minutes. Serve warm.

CDW

Cheese Zebras with Parmesan Ice Cream

These little pumpernickel stacks are a Dutch recipe and go very well with the eighteenth century Parmesan Ice, to form an interesting starter or even a savoury course. The Ice comes from the *Italian Confectioner* published in 1791. I like savoury ices but they are something that only have their vestigial remains in the champagne or mint sorbets served as an intercourse palate cleanser.

150g/6oz butter
2 hardboiled egg yolks, sieved
salt and freshly ground pepper
1 tsp Worcestershire sauce
150g/6oz mature Gouda cheese
4 slices pumpernickel bread

FOR THE PARMESAN ICE-CREAM:
55g/2oz granulated sugar
300ml/½ pint water
6 eggs, beaten
600ml/1 pint double cream
85g/3 oz Parmesan cheese

Beat the butter to a cream and add sieved yolks, salt, pepper, Worcestershire sauce and cheese. Spread the mixture on pumpernickel to the same thickness as the bread. Top with another slice of bread and repeat for 2 more layers. Wrap in cling film and chill for 2 hours or more. Cut in slices and serve with Parmesan Ice Cream.

To make the ice-cream, dissolve the sugar in the water in a small pan over a gentle heat. Then boil rapidly until the syrup has reduced to 300ml/½ pint. Add the eggs and cream and heat gently until the mixture thickens and comes to the boil. Mix in the cheese and pass through a sieve. Chill then freeze.

CDW

Aubergines in French Dressing

This is another simple way to treat aubergines and can be used as a salad, side dish or what you will. It is also a very good accompaniment to cold pink lamb.

2 large aubergines
salt and freshly ground pepper
8 tbsp olive oil
2 garlic cloves, crushed
2 tbsp lemon juice
1 tbsp sugar
1 level tsp cumin
chopped parsley

Cut the aubergines into 1cm/½inch thick slices, sprinkle with a little salt and leave for 30 minutes then wipe them dry with kitchen paper. Brush them generously with olive oil, sprinkle a little salt and pepper on the slices and grill until the flesh is tender. Make a marinade of what's left of the olive oil, garlic, lemon juice and cumin, mixing it well. Put the slices of aubergine in a serving dish, pour over the marinade, add a little salt and pepper and sprinkle over the parsley. Leave for several hours before serving.

JP

Potted Turkey

This recipe is the best way I know of using up left over turkey. I invented it at a demonstration a year ago in Ireland and the only reason it wasn't in the last book was I forgot about it. It freezes beautifully, and is perfect as a starter with toast or for sandwiches.

225g/8oz butter
900g/2lb turkey meat (both white and dark meat), cut into small pieces
juice of 1 lemon
1 scant tsp nutmeg
1 clove of garlic, crushed
½ tsp cayenne pepper
salt and freshly ground pepper

In a heavy frying pan melt the butter and lightly fry the garlic then throw in the turkey meat. Add all the seasonings and stir well. Taste and adjust the seasoning. Put into a food processor and blend to a coarse paste. This will store well in the refrigerator or in a pot covered with a layer of clarified butter. It will also freeze.

CDW

Spiced Pork Fillet

These little slices are a good thing to hand round with drinks to take the edge off the appetite. If used as a starter, you can dispense with the cocktails and eat them as you would salami, with the sauce on the side.

1 pork tenderloin, trimmed of sinew and fat
¼ cup soy sauce
1 clove of garlic, crushed
2 shallots, finely chopped
2 tbsp red wine
1 tbsp clear honey
2 tsp brown sugar
1 tsp grated fresh ginger
¼ tsp cinnamon
1 tbsp olive oil

Combine all the ingredients, except the pork and oil, in a glass or china bowl and mix them well. Place the loin of pork in this marinade and refrigerate for 3–4 hours, basting frequently or you can leave it overnight. When ready to cook, remove the pork and put it in an oiled roasting tin, reserve the marinade. Cook the pork in a preheated moderate oven 180°C/350°F/Gas 4 for about 45 minutes, turning and basting occasionally to get an all round roasting.

When cooked allow to cool and cut into thin slices and use cocktail sticks for picking up the slices. The marinade may be used as a dipping sauce; strain it, simmer it for 20 minutes and allow to cool.

JP

Meat Patties in Horseradish Sauce

I was surprised when I saw fresh horseradish on sale in Safeway – well done to them. I grow a lot of horseradish but always in a bucket or it takes over, just like mint. Grate the root in a food processor and you won't weep for days. The Scandinavians make much use of it, and this is a Swedish recipe. The Swedes are also fond of pickled beetroot but like it in a sweet pickle, not our harsh vinegar-based one.

2 medium onions, finely chopped
1 tbsp butter
450g/1lb steak, minced
1 medium potato, boiled and mashed
225g/8oz sweet pickled beetroot, grated
1 egg, beaten
3 tbsp milk
1 tbsp capers, finely chopped
salt and freshly ground pepper
oil for frying

FOR THE SAUCE:
300ml/10fl oz cream
salt
cayenne pepper
1 tbsp freshly grated horseradish

Fry the chopped onions in butter until soft and lightly browned. Mix them with the beef, potato, beetroot, egg, milk, capers and seasoning until well combined. Shape into 12 patties and refrigerate for 1 hour. Combine the sauce ingredients.

Heat the oil in a large heavy pan and fry the patties for 5–10 minutes until they are cooked to your liking. I like to drain off any excess oil from the pan and pour it over the patties to heat them through before serving. In Sweden the sauce is served on the side of the plate.

CDW

The Butt and Ben's Arbroath Crepe

Scotland's great legacy to food is cold smoking of fish and, when it comes to haddock, ingenuity knows no bounds. There are at least sixty-nine recorded variants on the theme including some which are sun-dried a patient version with Scots weather! Everyone knows the Arbroath smokie and it is such an old product that it is nice to think that Robert I's stirring declaration of independence at Arbroath in 1320 might have been composed over a supper of them. What most people don't know, however, is that the Arbroath smokie originated along the coast to Authmithie and only moved when the trade became too large. If you go to Authmithie you must go to that excellent little restaurant the Butt and Ben, this delicious crepe recipe is theirs.

FOR THE CREPE:
115g/4oz flour
pinch of baking powder
150ml/¼ pint full-cream milk
1 egg
pinch of salt

FOR THE FILLING:
1 pair of smokies
55g/2oz butter
300ml/½ pint double cream

Mix together the batter ingredients and leave to stand for 1 hour at least. Strip the flesh from the smokies and flake the meat. Heat in a pan the butter and cream to just below boiling point, throw in the flaked smokies and heat through.

Make 4 crepes with the batter and divide the smokie mixture equally between them, fold over and pour over the remaining sauce. Serve on hot plates.

CDW

Smoked Trout, Avocado and Shrimp Mousse

This is a very 1960s type of mousse, when the thrill of the avocado had just about reached us. However, it is always very good and I like to eat it with hot brown toast and a squeeze of lemon on the side.

2 fillets (225–275g/8–10oz) smoked trout
1 ripe avocado
300ml/1 pint crème fraîche
juice of ½ a lemon
2 tbsp finely grated lemon rind
150g/6oz cooked and shelled shrimps
salt and freshly ground black pepper

Skin and bone the trout, peel and stone the avocado and liquidise. Blend with crème fraîche, lemon juice, lemon rind, salt and pepper. Place half the mixture in a ramekin dish, cover with a layer of shrimps and then with the remaining mixture. Chill the mousse well before serving.

JP

Illustrated overleaf

Soused Herrings

The herring is probably one of the cheapest fish you can buy. It is also extremely good for you, providing essential oils. These soused herrings, probably originating in Denmark, make a good hors-d'oeuvre, which is improved by a dollop of sour cream.

4 herrings, cleaned, boned and heads and tails removed
1 small onion, sliced
2 bayleaves
150ml/¼ pint dry white wine
150ml/¼ pint good wine vinegar
1 tbsp mixed pickling sauce
salt and freshly ground pepper

Lay the herrings in a fireproof dish, cover with the sliced onion, sprinkle with the pickling spice and add bayleaves, salt and pepper. Mix the wine and wine vinegar and pour over. Cook in a preheated slow oven 150°C/300°F/Gas 2 for about 1½ hours. Allow to get cold before serving.

JP

Salmon Mousse with Cucumber Sauce

The use of blue cheese in this mousse means that it will lift even the blandest of farmed salmon. Clearly you don't want to use expensive wild salmon for this dish but use a good quality one. I cooked it for the barristers in the Lincoln's Inn programme and it was much admired. You can use any size mould, from small individual ones for a first course to very large ones for a buffet. If you don't overcook the fish or mess up with your gelatine it is foolproof.

450g/1lb salmon fillet
55g/2oz blue cheese
115g/4oz cream cheese
120ml/4fl oz sour cream
2 gerkins, finely chopped
1 stick celery, chopped
1 medium onion, finely chopped
salt
300ml/10fl oz cream, whipped
1 tbsp chopped dill
juice of ½ a lemon
1 sachet gelatine

FOR THE SAUCE:
1 cucumber
1 tbsp chopped chives
½ tsp sugar
1 tbsp white vinegar
150ml/5fl oz sour cream

Skin, bone and flake the salmon and put in a large mixing bowl. Mix the cheeses and the sour cream together then combine with the salmon and add the gerkins. Dissolve the gelatine following the packet instructions and blend into the salmon mixture. Add the remaining ingredients and mix well. Pour into wetted moulds and refrigerate for at least 2 hours, or until set.

To make the sauce, peel and de-seed the cucumber and chop finely. Mix with all ingredients except the cream and leave for 30 minutes then strain off the liquid and mix with the cream. Unmould the mousse and serve with the sauce.

CDW

Salmon Terrine

A salmon terrine is always a good thing to have up your sleeve in case unexpected guests arrive, especially on a Sunday after cocktails. Easy to make, it can be left in the refrigerator ready to pounce on when necessary.

750g/1½ lb raw salmon, boned and skinned
2 tbsp chopped shallot
4 tbsp dry white wine
225g/½lb whiting or any white fish, boned and skinned
150g/6oz breadcrumbs, soaked in milk and squeezed dry
85g/3oz butter, softened
1 tbsp chopped parsley
2 tsp chopped and blanched chives
¼ tsp nutmeg
salt and freshly ground pepper
1 whole egg and 2 egg yolks, beaten

Cut 450g/1lb of salmon into finger-size pieces and place in a glass dish. Sprinkle with the shallot, salt and pepper to taste and white wine. Place the rest of the salmon, the white fish and breadcrumbs in a food processor and blend together. Add 55g/2oz of butter, parsley, chives and nutmeg and bind the whole lot together with the beaten eggs.

Butter a terrine dish with the remaining butter, put a layer of the forcemeat on the bottom, cover with a layer of salmon fingers, add forcemeat and continue in this fashion until the ingredients are finished. Strain the marinade on to the terrine, put the lid on the terrine and cook in a bain marie in a preheated slow oven at 160°C/325°F/Gas 3 for 1½–2 hours. Leave to get cold.

JP

Rabbit Pâté

For all that is talked about lean meat, rabbit is still scorned and the wastage of this good and healthy meat every year is immense. I like a delicate rabbit pâté much better than a chicken one, the flavour is real and it is a lot safer.

900g/2lb raw rabbit meat
900g/2lb pork
450g/1lb fat bacon
2 onions, peeled
1 tbsp parsley, finely chopped
2 tsp thyme
3 liqueur glasses brandy
salt and freshly ground pepper
bottle of cornichons (small gherkins)
1 bayleaf
225g/8oz thin rashers of streaky bacon

Coarsely mince or process the rabbit, pork, bacon and onions together, add the other ingredients (except the bayleaf and bacon) and mix, using your hands, until they are all well amalgamated. Half fill an earthenware terrine with the rabbit mixture, then put in a double layer of cornichons. Fill to the top with more mixture, place the bayleaf on top, cover with bacon rashers cut into thin strips and press down well. Add a layer of greaseproof paper. Cover and cook in a bain marie in a preheated slow oven at 150°C/300°F/Gas 2 for 1 hour for small terrines, 2 hours if large. To store, pour over a layer of melted lard and cover with a piece of waxed paper. Store in a cool place for a month or more.

CDW

FISH AND SHELLFISH

*The ladies receive some direction at Kylemore Abbey in western
Ireland, with the Mother Abbess looking on*

I am tempted to say unless you have a good fish-monger don't bother. As Jennifer says, if it smells of fish it isn't fresh. Moreover you can talk to your fishmonger: I have been in pursuit of gulls' eggs since the year began and my own dear Mr Clarke found them for me. When I went to collect them he was extolling the virtues of an 11-stone halibut caught off the west coast so I bought some of that too. This set me thinking. When I was young a fish that size was the norm, turbot were huge monsters and a cod was a denizen of the depths, but nowadays over-fishing has destroyed all that. A Hong Kong lawyer was telling me recently that the waters around Asia are all fished out and Mr Doyle, the owner of

Sydney's most famous seafood restaurant, had been on television predicting a day when Australians would no longer be able to afford to buy their own seafood because of the Asian Maw. It makes me think that supermarkets should be banned from selling what they don't know how to look after properly, and mass-produced frozen fish concoctions should be banned too, to prevent waste of this diminishing asset.

I like to serve a separate fish course at a dinner party but most people will have it as a main course. It is a good choice if you are eating late as it is easily digestible and takes no time to cook. Filming at a convent in Galway on the west coast of Ireland took me back to my child-

Taking a break from all that cooking

hood, when I used to visit cousins on the Donegal coast. We would go and fish for mackerel from an old dinghy, and how good they tasted fresh from the sea. So too did the fish we caught from the line trailed behind the Caribbean yacht I worked on, hauling them into the boat in a hurry before the sharks could get at them. Nowhere in Great Britain is far from the sea and yet you find fresher fish in the hill towns of inland Spain than we can. In this age of activists I wish you would all go out and protest for fresher, safer products rather than just not buying what is available.

The trick with fish is to make your guests wait for it rather than the other way round. I never understand people who want everything cooked before people arrive – some of my most pleasant dalliances have been conducted in my kitchen during a dinner party! And anyway I'm not that keen on casseroles. In this age of fisharians (i.e. vegetarians who eat fish) the ability to cook it well is of great importance, we are always being

told how good oily fish is for us and eating it is so much nicer than swallowing a spoonful of cod liver oil. It is also important to try the different range of fish available. So many people just stick to cod, haddock or salmon, but don't be afraid to experiment and ask your fishmonger what is particularly good or in season – remember fish have seasons, just like fruit and vegetables.

In Connemara Jennifer cooked lobster and we had great fun tracking the local lobster king from the quay to the pub, as one might expect in Ireland. We found him sitting happily quaffing his Guinness with a wooden box containing six live lobsters by his side. They were beautiful lobsters and the nuns did them justice, but sadly the ones we ate in our hotel were overcooked, and overcooked fish is a sin against heaven.

In the grounds of Kylemore Abbey, with a tranquil view over the water

Fish Stew

You can use any fish in this receipt but I flavour the fleshier ones such as monk, coley and red mullet which all give a good flavour. Ask your fishmonger to fillet and clean them. If you like you can add spoonfuls of aioli to the finished stew, once in the bowl.

750g/1½lb assorted fish, cut into chunks
1 tbsp olive oil
25g/1oz butter
1 large onion, chopped
1 large leek, white part only, chopped
2 celery sticks, de-fibred and chopped
2 cloves of garlic, finely chopped
115g/¼lb mushrooms, finely sliced
2 potatoes, peeled and chopped
3 large tomatoes, skinned and chopped
150ml/5fl oz white wine
300ml/10fl oz water
1 bouquet garni
2 bayleaves
salt and freshly ground pepper
1 tbsp chopped parsley
pinch of saffron

Fry onion, leek, celery, garlic, mushrooms and potatoes in the oil and butter until the onion begins to brown. Add the chopped tomatoes. Add the fish. Cover with wine and water. Add the bouquet garni, bayleaves and salt and pepper to taste. Bring to the boil and simmer for 12–15 minutes. Add the parsley and the saffron before serving.

JP

Fish with Egg and Lemon Sauce

This is a very comforting dish with the traditional Greek Avoglemoni sauce. If you can't go to my fishmonger, Mr Clarke, find one nearby and make a friend of him and then you can be sure of getting really fresh fish. It will be better than the ammoniac stuff which you follow your nose to in some supermarkets.

4 fish steaks
2–3 sticks celery or equivalent celeriac
3 tbsp olive oil
25g/1oz butter
1 small onion, finely sliced
4 tbsp white wine
150ml/¼ pint water
chopped dill or parsley
salt and freshly ground pepper

FOR THE SAUCE:
2 egg yolks
juice of 1 lemon

Poach the celery or celeriac in boiling salted water for 4 minutes and drain. Heat the olive oil and butter in a heavy pan and sauté the onion until gilded but not brown. Add the wine and the water and bring to the boil, add the celery and mix well. Cover and cook gently for 5 minutes.

Add the fish and spoon over the mixture. The fish should be half immersed in the liquid, if not add a little more water. Cover and simmer gently for about 10–15 minutes, until the fish feels tender but is not overcooked. Remove from the heat and keep warm. Let it stand for 5 minutes while you make the sauce.

Using a fork beat the egg yolks with a tablespoon of water for 2 minutes, add the lemon juice and beat for a further minute. Add (one at a time) 4–5 tablespoons of juice from the fish, stirring well with a wooden spoon. Pour the sauce over the fish and shake the saucepan well to distribute. Sprinkle on dill or parsley, season to taste and return to a very low heat for 2–3 minutes, stirring gently until it thickens and taking care not to break the fish. Serve with new potatoes and a green salad.

CDW

Cod Fillet in Mushroom, Shrimp and Cheese Sauce

Far from being the cheapest fish as it was not so many years ago, cod has now reached its rightful place in the menus of every grand restaurant.

4 thick cod fillets
115g/4oz butter
55g/2oz plain flour
300ml/½ pint milk
300ml/½ pint fish stock
115g/4oz mushrooms, halved
85g/3oz strong Cheddar cheese, grated
1 tsp anchovy essence
1 tbsp chopped parsley
salt and freshly ground pepper
225g/8oz cooked shrimps

Melt half the butter in a saucepan, add the flour, stir, and allow to bubble for 2 or 3 minutes, but be careful not to let it burn. Remove from heat. Butter a baking dish with 12g/½oz butter and place the cod fillets in it, cover with the fish stock and cook in a preheated moderate oven 190°C/370°F/Gas 5 for 15 minutes. Strain off the fish stock, add to the milk and gradually add this to the saucepan containing the flour and butter. Bring slowly to the boil, stirring gently, to get a smooth consistency.

Sauté the mushrooms in the remaining butter, add to your sauce with 25g/1oz of the cheese and the anchovy essence. Stir until cheese has melted, season to taste. Cut the fish into bite-size pieces. Add the shrimps and parsley to the fish in the baking dish, pour the sauce over the fish shaking the dish gently for the sauce to sink. Place the dish in a preheated oven at 200°C/400°F/Gas 6 for 10 minutes. Sprinkle over the remaining cheese, and put under a hot grill for a few minutes for the cheese to melt and brown.

JP

Smoked Haddock and Lovage Tart

This recipe comes from *Feasting on Herbs,* an excellent book by my dear friend Sue Lawrence who is one of the best cooks I know. I cooked it untested for a dinner of Gaelic poets and it was much praised by the late great Sorley Maclean. As he was speaking Gaelic at the time I can't tell you what he said. It is excellent, and I know you will love it.

FOR THE PASTRY:
150g/6oz plain flour
55g/2oz polenta
salt
115g/4oz unsalted butter
1 egg combined
1 tbsp olive oil

FOR THE FILLING:
350g/12 oz undyed smoked haddock
150ml/¼ pint milk
150ml/¼ pint cream
3 eggs
2 tbsp lovage
salt and freshly ground pepper

To make your pastry in a food processor, mix all the dried ingredients, chop in the butter then add the egg and oil, spinning until a paste forms. Chill for 30 minutes. Roll out and line a 23cm/9in flan tin. The pastry will be very crumbly so patch it in by hand and chill in the tin for a further 30 minutes. Bake blind in a preheated oven 190°C/375°F/Gas 5 until the pastry is cooked and pale gold, 15–20 minutes. Cool slightly.

Poach fish in the milk, remove from milk and flake into pie crust reserving the milk. Whisk the cream and eggs into the milk and add the lovage, season and pour over the fish. Return to the oven and bake for 30 minutes or until the filling is set. Cool slightly before serving. This is also good cold.

CDW

Hake Portuguese

Both the Portuguese and the Spanish have a passion for hake. It is a very good fish though not used much by the British – pray go out and buy some. It is also very good cold, covered in mayonnaise and served with a beautiful potato salad.

4 x 225g/½lb cuts of hake
115g/4oz butter
2 tbsp olive oil
8 shallots, finely chopped
450g/1lb tomatoes, skinned, de-seeded and chopped
1 yellow pepper, skinned, de-seeded and chopped
1 tbsp frozen peas
115g/4oz cooked (al dente) rice
2 tbsp chopped parsley
2 glasses white wine
salt and freshly ground pepper

Heat 25g/1oz butter with the olive oil in an ovenproof dish, add the shallots and fry until the shallots are translucent. Lay the fish on top of the cooked shallots and dot with knobs of the remaining butter. Cover the fish with chopped tomatoes, yellow pepper, frozen peas and surround the fish with the rice and chopped parsley. Pour in the wine, add salt and pepper and bake in a moderate oven at 190°C/375°F/Gas 5/ for 30–35 minutes.

JP

Halibut Burger with Anchovy Aioli

This is another Swedish dish and a good use for the excellent halibut coming onto the market. My Mr Clarke gets it line-caught from the Orkneys although just recently he has been getting some good fish from the Firth of Forth which is good news for Edinburghers. If you don't like the Swedish version of aioli make it the ordinary way.

750g/1½lb halibut fillet
salt and freshly ground pepper
55g/2oz butter
8 slices country bread

FOR AIOLI:
3 small potatoes
3 egg yolks
175g/6fl oz olive oil
1 clove of garlic, crushed
5 anchovy fillets, chopped
tomato relish
1 red onion

To make the aioli, boil and mash potatoes, cool and combine with egg yolks. Add a few drops of olive oil in a thin stream, whisking all the time until all the oil is mixed in. Mix the garlic and anchovies into the aioli.

Divide the fish into 4 pieces, season with salt and pepper and fry in the butter for about 1 minute each side. Grill the bread, smear with tomato relish. Put a piece of fish between each two pieces of bread and dab on some aioli, place a piece of red onion on top.

CDW

Singapore Prawns with Bugis Street Sauce

I haven't been back to Singapore since 1948 but I always remember those marvellous prawn dishes I had in Bugis Street. This recipe is the nearest I can get to one of the sauces. There was always a side dish of small red chillies and one of our friends would chew these as if he was eating peanuts. The more reserved of us would take one or two.

750g/1½lb cooked and shelled prawns
2 tbsp vegetable oil
115g/4oz mushrooms, sliced
4 tbsp chopped spring onions
1 clove of garlic, chopped
1 tsp grated fresh ginger
1½ tbsp hoison sauce
1½ tbsp oyster sauce
2 tsp red Thai curry paste
pinch of five spice powder
300ml/10fl oz coconut milk
salt and pepper

Heat the vegetable oil in wok or frying pan, put in the mushrooms, spring onions, garlic and ginger for a couple of minutes. Add the hoisin sauce, oyster sauce, red curry paste and five spice powder and stir well. Then add the coconut milk, a little salt and pepper and the prawns. Simmer gently for 1–2 minutes and serve on a bed of rice or noodles.

JP

Caper-Stuffed Herring with Warm Potato Salad

I have no time for people who purport to listen to the health pundits and then eat cod-liver oil capsules as their answer to oily fish. I love herrings – the food history of our coastal areas is ripe with herring stories and accounts of the indomitable herring wives who followed the shoals of fish round the country. This is a Swedish dish and an excellent way of cooking your herring.

55g/2oz capers
2 tbsp chopped chives
2 tbsp dill
1 tbsp freshly grated horseradish
85g/3oz cream cheese
6 herrings, boned but still connected along the back fin
salt and pepper

FOR THE SALAD:
7 rashers of bacon chopped
6 cold boiled small potatoes, roughly chopped
2 shallots or small onion, finely chopped
wine vinegar
olive oil
1 tbsp capers

Chop the capers and mix with the chives, dill and horseradish. Add the cream cheese and season to taste. Dry the fish fillets, lay filling on one side and fold over so the fish looks whole.

Fry the bacon in a heavy pan till crisp, add potatoes and heat through, remove to a dish and stir in the raw onion. Pour over the vinegar and a little olive oil, season and mix well. Keep warm.

Rub the fish with a little oil, heat the pan, it must be very hot. Fry the fish for about 2 minutes each side. Serve with the potato salad, garnished with capers.

CDW

Monkfish and Baked Potato Kebabs

This is a quirky kebab but one I think you will enjoy. We have talked before of gigot of monkfish, so why not a kebab!

450g/1lb trimmed monkfish
2 large potatoes
salt and freshly ground pepper
2 tbsp olive oil
2 tbsp butter
juice of ½ a lemon
55g/2oz strong Cheddar
85ml/3fl oz sour cream
1 tbsp oil

Rub the potatoes with salt and oil and bake for 1 hour in a preheated hot oven at 220°C/425°F/Gas 7. Cut the monkfish into 2.5cm/1 inch chunks. Heat the olive oil and butter and sauté the fish until just cooked through, about 5 minutes, season with lemon juice. Slice the potatoes carefully widthways to leave each piece intact. Thread alternate pieces of fish and potato on pre-soaked wooden or metal kebab skewers and place on a heatproof dish. Mix together the cheese and the sour cream and season. Ladle over the kebabs and sear under a very hot grill until the cheese bubbles, serve at once.

CDW

Coconut Salmon

This is a dish I invented when demonstrating at the Highland Show with the mad boys from Herbie's Delicatessen in Edinburgh. I happened to have a lot of creamed coconut in my store cupboard and thought it would be an interesting experiment. I was delighted with the result.

4 fillets salmon, skinned
85g/3oz creamed coconut
150ml/¼ pint hot water
1 shallot
1 clove garlic, finely chopped
1cm/½ inch fresh ginger, finely chopped
½ tsp ground cardamom
½ tsp cumin
salt and freshly ground black pepper

Dissolve the coconut in the hot water and add the shallot, garlic and ginger. Rub the cumin, cardamom and black pepper into the salmon fillets and set aside for at least 30 minutes. Pour the coconut mixture into a sauté pan and simmer until reduced by half. Add salt to taste and the salmon fillets, turning to coat with sauce. Cook for 6–8 minutes and serve.

CDW

Salmon Cutlets with Leeks and Cream

This is a good idea for using farmed salmon, which is cheaper than the wild but can do with extra flavouring. The leeks go well with the fish without overpowering it. Very suitable for a visiting maiden aunt, of which I am one.

4 salmon cutlets
4 medium-sized leeks, finely chopped
115g/4oz butter
300ml/½ pint double cream, whipped not too stiffly
225g/8oz cooked prawns
juice of ½ a lemon
salt and pepper
tin foil

Melt 85g/3oz butter in a frying pan and sauté the finely chopped leeks over a low heat until soft. Smear 4 tin foil sheets large enough to loosely enclose each cutlet and leek, with the remaining butter. Place a generous layer of leek in the centre of each sheet, add a salmon cutlet, another layer of leek and top with a generous dollop of cream and 55g/2oz prawns. Sprinkle about 1 teaspoon of lemon juice over the top. Bring the edges of the tin foil together and make into a parcel so that none of the juices will run out. Place the parcels on a baking tray and cook in a preheated medium oven at 190°C/375°F/Gas 5 for 25 minutes.

JP

Salmon in Red Pepper Sauce

You all know how to peel red peppers I'm sure. Char them over a flame or under a grill, then put them immediately in a plastic bag and allow them to cool, and the skin slides off easily. Do not make the mistake a well known cookery writer once made, in front of a large audience, of trying to peel them straight from the flame. She was unable to do a book signing for me as we had no gloves to cover the Acriflex. The egg white gives a bit more body to the sauce.

900g/2lb tranch of salmon
2 red peppers
2 garlic cloves
salt and freshly ground pepper
1 egg white
120ml/4fl oz fish stock
1 wine glass red wine

Peel the peppers and purée them with the garlic cloves and a pinch of salt until smooth, add the egg white and process again. Season the salmon and poach it covered in the stock and wine. Remove fish, reduce stock and add the red pepper mixture, heat through gently and serve with fish.

CDW

Roasted Salmon with Scallops and Mustard Butter

I can't tell you how good this is. I was introduced to it by Guy Harrington, one of our dear researchers, who in his day ran many a restaurant or strummed the piano in far off bars. We had it as a starter, but it could be a splendid main course with a few new potatoes.

900g/2lb salmon middle cut, boned, or fillets
150g/6oz butter
8 scallops, without roe
3 generous tsp wholegrain mustard
4 level tsp dried dill weed, or
2 tsp each of dried and fresh dill
salt and freshly ground pepper
275g/10oz fresh spinach or rocket

Preheat the oven to 230°C/450°F/Gas 8. Place the salmon piece or fillets skin-side up in a shallow ovenproof dish. Cook in the oven for 15 minutes. Meanwhile gently melt the butter in a small saucepan. Remove from the heat and stir in the mustard and dill. Season to taste. Remove the salmon from the oven and place the scallops round it, baste with the mustard sauce. Return to the oven for a further 5 minutes. Slice the salmon quite thickly and serve on top of the spinach or rocket and spoon over the mustard butter.

JP

Illustrated overleaf

Marrow Stuffed with Salmon

This dish was inspired by a letter from my Hungarian barrister friend John Zeigler who wrote to admonish me on my misrepresentation of Rigo Jancsi chocolate slices. In the letter he referred to a Hungarian way of serving marrow with salmon. This isn't it but it is a fun dish all the same.

225g/8oz salmon
salt and freshly ground pepper
55g/2oz cooked rice
1 tbsp chopped pickled cucumber
1 tbsp sour cream
1 tbsp chopped dill
1 medium-sized marrow
25g/1oz butter

In a frying pan briefly sauté the salmon until you can flake it. Season well. Mix the salmon with the other ingredients. Cut a cap from the broad end of the marrow and hollow out, removing the seeds and some flesh. Rub the inside of the marrow with pepper. Fill with the filling. Replace the cap and secure with some tin foil. Place in a baking dish, brush with butter, cover with foil and bake in a preheated oven at 180°C/350°F/Gas 4 for 1–1½ hours.

CDW

Baked Stuffed Sewin

Sewin may be more familiar to you by its other name, sea trout. To my mind it is even better than salmon. It is a good natural fish with a very delicate flavour and it can be bought in different sizes according to your needs. It is very good just plain with a sauce verte, but this receipt is a little more exciting and has my beloved anchovy fillets within.

4 sewin, weighing about 450g/1lb each, filleted
8 tbsp white breadcrumbs
150ml/¼ pint milk
150g/6oz shallots, finely chopped
6 mushrooms, stalks removed and chopped small
150g/6oz butter
1 egg
2 tbsp chopped parsley
juice of ½ a lemon
pinch of grated nutmeg
salt and freshly ground pepper
4 anchovy fillets soaked in milk for 30 minutes

Ask your fishmonger to fillet the sewin. Soak the breadcrumbs in the milk, then squeeze the breadcrumbs out and set aside. Gently fry the shallots and mushrooms in 115g/4oz butter, until the shallots become translucent. Mix the breadcrumbs with egg, chopped parsley, lemon juice, grated nutmeg, salt and pepper and add to the mushroom mixture. Stuff the mixture into the 4 sewin fillets, adding 1 anchovy to each. Wrap each one in tin foil. Grease an ovenproof dish with the rest of the butter, add the foil-wrapped fillets and bake in a preheated moderate oven at 190°C/375°F/Gas 5 for 40 minutes.

JP

Lobster with Latkas

I have an unlimited passion for lobsters which I do very well with, thanks to my dear Mr Clarke of Fisher Row, Musselburgh, the best fishmonger in Britain. I also love latkas, those crispy mouth watering Jewish potato pancakes. So it seemed to me an excellent idea to combine the two.

4 boiled lobsters
85g/3oz butter
115g/4oz shallots, sliced
140g/5oz mushrooms, sliced
150ml/¼ pint whisky
freshly ground black pepper
pinch of ground cloves
300ml/½ pint double cream

FOR LATKAS:
900g/2lb potatoes, peeled and finely grated
225g/8oz onion, grated
150g/6oz matzo meal, use flour if not available
4 eggs
2 tsp caraway seeds
salt and freshly ground pepper
oil for frying

Remove the meat from the lobsters and cut into pieces. Melt 55g/2oz butter and fry the shallots until soft, add the mushrooms and cook gently, then add the lobster and mix well. Cover and cook very gently for 3 minutes. Warm the whisky, set it alight and, when the flames have died down, pour over the lobster. Season with black pepper and cloves and add the cream. Shake over the heat until well-mixed, cover and cook over a very gentle flame for 5 minutes.

To make the latkas, wash the grated potatoes in several changes of cold water to remove excess starch. Pat dry with a towel and mix with the rest of the ingredients. Season well. Heat the oil in a large frying pan, drop tablespoons of the mixture into the hot oil. Flatten each dollop into a round small flat pancake. Fry on medium heat for 3–4 minutes on each side until the pancake is a pale golden brown and perfectly crisp. Drain on absorbent paper and serve very hot with the lobster. If you are being stylish you can stack the latkas with lobster sandwiched between and the sauce drizzled round the base of the stack.

CDW

Lobster with Mayonnaise

When making the mayonnaise, it is essential that all the ingredients are at room temperature. The eggs should not be stored in the fridge as they will curdle when making the mayonnaise.

1 lobster per serving
1 egg yolk
Dijon mustard
salt
pepper
light extra virgin olive oil

FOR 300ML/½ PINT OF MAYONNAISE:
300ml/½ pint olive oil/sunflower oil/mixture of the two
2 egg yolks
salt and freshly ground black pepper
1 level teaspoon of Dijon mustard
lemon juice/white wine vinegar, according to taste

Fill a pan with luke warm water and place it on a hotplate. Place the lobster in the pan and cover. Once the water has come to the boil, cook the lobster for ten minutes or until they no longer have any blue hue and have turned a deep red-orange colour.

Remove the lobster from the pan and leave to cool. Once cool you can prepare the lobster in the traditional manner: with a sharp knife make an incision at the point where the head joins the body and cut down the length of the lobster towards the tail. Make sure that you have cut right the way through the body. Now turn the lobster 180 degrees and cut from the original incision back through the head. With your fingers gradually prise the shell apart so that it falls into two halves. Remove the front claws and set aside. With your index finger prise the meat out of the shell (trying to keep it in one piece, again working from the tail upwards. Replace the meat in the shell (this process makes it easier for your guests to keep their fingers clean) and repeat with the second half. Using a cleaver or hammer crack both sides of the claws. Remove the surrounding shell and extract the meat in a single piece. Arrange the two halves of lobster on a plate together with the claw meat and serve with mayonnaise, which you can make in the following way:

Put eggs, mustard, pinch of salt, grinding of pepper and a small squeeze of lemon juice/vinegar in a basin and beat well with a wooden spoon or beater. Start adding the oil, drop by drop to begin with, stirring all the time. When the mixture starts to emulsify you may add more oil in steady dribblets but keep stirring until you get the required jelly-like substance, which is the consistency that proper mayonnaise should be. Finally test for more seasoning.

JP

Baked Sole with Horseradish

I love horseradish and clearly from the way old plantings of it still grow round ancient dwellings it was once more generally used. It is an excellent digestive, but in British cooking its use really only survives with beef whereas in Scandinavia and Central Europe it is used much more extensively. This is a Polish recipe given to me by an old lady in whose Sussex lake we used to fish as children.

8 fillets of sole, plaice or haddock
salt
1 tbsp white wine vinegar
25g/1oz melted butter
sugar
115g/4oz grated horseradish
1 sharp apple, peeled, cored and shredded
175ml/6 fl oz soured cream

Sprinkle the fish with salt and vinegar. Place in a buttered dish and dot with melted butter. Bake in a preheated oven 200°C/400°F/Gas 6 for 10 minutes. Mix the horseradish, apple and soured cream together. Season with salt and sugar. Pour this mixture over the fish and bake for another 10 minutes. Serve with boiled potatoes.

CDW

Sole in Vermouth

Vermouth is always good with fish, having a stronger flavour than any white wine and, as I'm not tempted to drink it on its own, I always seem to have some. Sole is one of the finest fish but alas now very expensive. However, we all deserve a great treat every now and then. So enjoy.

8 fillets of sole
3 shallots, finely chopped
150g/6oz butter
2 tbsp parsley, finely chopped
1 tbsp fresh tarragon
dry vermouth
juice of ½ a lemon
salt and freshly ground pepper

Soften shallots in 55g/2oz of butter in a large ovenproof dish and add parsley and tarragon. Place fish fillets on top of shallots and herbs and season with salt and pepper. Pour in sufficient vermouth to come level with the fish. Dot fish with 55g/2oz butter. Cook in preheated hot oven at 220°C/425°F/Gas 7 for 20–30 minutes or until the fish flakes easily.

Remove the fish to hot serving dish, pour juices into a saucepan and reduce rapidly to half. Remove the pan from the heat and whisk in remaining butter, taste for seasoning, add a squeeze of lemon juice and pour the sauce over fish.

JP

Trout with Olives, Orange, Tomato and Vermouth

I originally invented this dish to go with pheasant, but people kept bringing me trout so I thought I'd give it a try and it works equally well with either. Men who shoot often fish as well so the versatility will be appreciated by those who have to handle the spoils!

5 trout
4 rashers bacon
12 shallots
55g/2oz butter
salt and freshly ground pepper
12 black olives
4 green olives
50ml/2oz stock
1 wine glass of vermouth
juice of 1 orange
small can tomato juice

Sauté bacon and shallots in the butter. Add the trout, season well and cook for 5 minutes. Add the olives, vermouth, orange and tomato juices and cook till done, about 10 minutes.

CDW

Trout in Rosé de Loire

A lovely pink trout with a lovely pink sauce. A very suitable dish for mid Lent or a mid Advent Sunday when priests always wear pink vestments.

4 medium sized trout, boned and gutted
115g/4oz butter
4 shallots, chopped
600ml/1 pint Rosé de Loire
1 bouquet garni
salt and freshly ground pepper
4 egg yolks
300ml/½ pint double cream
1 tbsp pink lumpfish
1 tbsp croûtons

Ask the fishmonger to gut and bone the trout. Melt half the butter in a frying pan and gently sauté the chopped shallots, do not burn. Add the trout and cook gently until lightly brown on both sides. Butter an ovenproof dish with half the remaining butter. Place the trout in the dish, add the wine, bouquet garni, salt and pepper. Dot each fish with knobs of the remaining butter and cook in a medium preheated oven 180°C/350°F/Gas 4 for 25–30 minutes, basting once or twice. Place fish on a serving plate and keep warm.

Pour the residual juices into a small saucepan and boil rapidly until reduced by half. Allow to cool for 2 minutes. Whisk the egg yolks with the cream and slowly add the juices while continuing to whisk. When the mixture is light and frothy, pour over the fish and serve immediately, garnished with lumpfish roe and croûtons.

JP

Trout Quenelles with Watercress Sauce

Although as my friend Angus quite rightly, if somewhat acerbically pointed out, the French only make *quenelles* with pike, trout is an excellent substitute. It is also one which I served at a ten-course dinner party I once cooked in an alcoholic blackout so you can see that it is not difficult.

275g/10oz fresh trout
275g/10oz smoked trout
3 egg whites
a pinch of mace
salt and pepper
300ml/½ pint double cream

FOR THE SAUCE:
5 tbsp finely chopped shallot
150ml/¼ pint dry white wine
150ml/¼ pint strong chicken stock
300ml/½ pint whipping cream
4 bunches watercress
lemon juice to taste
55g/2oz butter

Put into a food processor all the fish and blend until smooth, add the egg whites and blend until completely smooth. Add salt and pepper and mace, pour in the cream with the machine running, do not run the machine for more than 20 seconds. Don't let the mixture get too thin, it must sit up on a spoon. Chill for 30 minutes.

Bring a wide pan of salted water to a simmer. Dip a dessertspoon in warm water and take a good rounded spoonful of the mixture. Use another spoon to form the quenelle. Poach each quenelle in the water for 8–10 minutes, remove with a slotted spoon and drain on kitchen paper. Put in a warm dish and when all are made pour over sauce and serve at once.

To make the sauce, simmer the shallot and the wine together for 15 minutes or more until it forms a soft purée and the wine is almost evaporated. Add stock and cream, season and boil until reduced by one third and coating a spoon. Pick over the watercress discarding tough stalks and discoloured leaves and toss into a pan of boiling salted water. Blanch for 2–3 minutes, drain and refresh under a cold tap. Squeeze out excess water. In the food processor purée the watercress for 1–2 minutes until a smooth purée is formed, pour the hot cream over the purée and process adding the lemon juice and the butter in small pieces. Strain and reheat without boiling, pour over quenelles and serve at once.

CDW

Fresh Grilled Tuna Salad

During a shoot we tend to eat rather a lot and rather late. There is nothing I like more on my return to my flat in Victoria than a simple salad Niçoise. I always feel that there is something very restorative about it.

1 tuna steak per person, about 2.5cm/1 inch thick
olive oil
350g/12oz baby new potatoes
115g/4oz green beans
10 lettuce leaves – Cos or similar
3 hard-boiled eggs, quartered
225g/8oz cherry tomatoes
8 anchovy fillets
12 black olives
1 red onion, thickly sliced
55g/2oz salted butter
3 garlic cloves
1 tbsp balsamic vinegar
4–5 tbsp olive oil
2 tbsp chopped chervil
salt and pepper

You can grill the tuna but it is far better cooked on a griddle, turn both ways to achieve that criss-cross pattern. Grill or griddle the tuna for about 1½ minutes in total, so that it is still pink in the middle. If you prefer it well done, cook for 1½ minutes each side. Par-boil the baby potatoes and then sauté in a pan with the butter and one clove of garlic until golden. Pour the oil into a jug and add the rest of the garlic, chervil, and salt and pepper. Slowly whisk in the balsamic vinegar and stand the mixture aside. Boil the beans for 3½ minutes. Drain and run under cold water. Chop the beans in half. Place the tomatoes, the potatoes and the beans and the red onion into a salad bowl and drizzle half the vinaigrette onto this. Toss thoroughly and serve with the tuna steak on top of the salad.

JP

MEAT

'Don't worry dear, I won't eat you.' ... but do we believe Jennifer?

Since our last volume I am happy to report that a number of vegetarians have been restored to the fold of meat eaters. I have never been able to understand the reasoning that if you don't like the way meat is reared or killed you turn vegetarian. Surely you should stand up and fight for changes and support the organic trade rather than risk your life with a paraquat-fed Third World carrot. Anyone who saw the quality of the Prince of Wales cattle herd when we filmed at Highgrove, and observed how happy and confident they were, would agree with me.

Jennifer has made the point that you can't really digest pork without its fat, but people forget this when buying meat. I spoke recently to a pig farmer who was telling me that the supermarkets are demanding leaner and leaner beasts and as a result the pigs have no natural protection against extremes of weather and get sunburnt very easily. We filmed with a lot of very happy Gloucester Old Spot pigs in the Cotswolds and it was great to see the boar and the sow lying about soaking up the sun, when they weren't trying to push Spike our cameraman off the bucket on which he was standing to film. Jennifer and I were taking bets on whether he would join them in the mud, but he managed to stay on his perch. The farmer said that the young pigs needed a mud wallow to escape the danger of sunburn, which makes me worry for those so called happy

Happy Gloucester Old Spots out in the mud

*Clarissa hands out the rosettes at the pony
club gymkhana*

pigs standing around in shadeless fields.

What a wealth of variety we have lost with the unification of breeds of sheep. Recently I was preparing a lunch for the Duke of Hamilton and his Trustees at Lennoxlove House, where I am the in-house caterer, and complained to my butcher, Colin Peat of Haddington, that the chops he was offering were too large for what I required. 'Well,' he replied, 'we'll just have to take them from a black-face sheep, they'll be smaller!'

Mutton is a strong flavour and we live increasingly in a country where the only accept-able strong flavour is a vindaloo curry. Curiously the only people in Britain who really still eat mutton are the Asian community. I was interest-ed to see on the menu in a Birmingham balti house both curried lamb and curried mutton; elsewhere we have lost such distinctions of palate. What a bland and tasteless world we are heading towards so terrifyingly fast.

Our views on beef are well-known, and I don't want to bore you with reiteration, so I shall merely make the point that British beef is now the safest in the world. For one of the pro-grammes in the last series we cooked a splendid wing rib of beef from the Duke of Buccleugh's excellent outlet for the Gurkhas (as the men are Hindus and don't eat beef it wasn't our most tact-ful choice, but the officers were mostly British so it was okay). What a shame that when we went to Smithfield this year we couldn't buy the same cut on the bone.

Pot Roast of Beef

This is a welcome winter dish which fills the house with delicious aromas. Try to get a well-hung joint of beef – it goes without saying, so I'll say it, the better the meat the better the pot roast.

900g/2lb rump beef, topside preferably
salt and freshly ground pepper
150g/6oz pork fat lardons
1.75 litres/1½ pints beef stock
16 button onions
4 carrots, sliced
115g/4oz mushrooms
2 tomatoes, peeled, de-seeded and quartered
1 tsp sugar

FOR THE MARINADE:
1 large onion, sliced
2 carrots, sliced
1 small turnip, chopped
2 cloves
bouquet garni
1 clove of garlic, crushed
8 peppercorns
2 tbsp olive oil
2 tbsp wine vinegar
600ml/1 pint white wine

Rub meat with salt and pepper and place in a non-metallic bowl. Combine the ingredients for the marinade, pour over the meat and refrigerate for 12–24 hours turning occasionally. Remove meat from the marinade and dry thoroughly with kitchen paper. Strain the vegetables from the marinade and reserve both.

Fry the lardons in a frying pan, add the marinated vegetables and cook until lightly golden. Remove the vegetables with a slotted spoon and put in the bottom of a casserole. Brown the meat in the hot pork fat on all sides and place on top of the vegetables. Pour a little of the fat out of the frying pan and reserve. Add the marinade to the frying pan, boil briskly and stir with a wooden spoon. Transfer to a saucepan, scraping out any bits with a wooden spoon. Add the beef stock and bring to the boil and boil briskly for a few minutes, then pour it over the beef in the casserole. Add more stock if it does not come up to half the side of the beef. Bake in a preheated slow oven at 150°C/300°F/Gas 2 for 2½ hours.

Meanwhile, sauté the carrots gently in the reserved pork fat, remove when cooked, then sauté the button onions and mushrooms; finally add the chopped tomatoes and sugar. Set aside.

Remove the beef from the casserole, mash the casseroled vegetables and strain this stock through a fine sieve, discarding the mashed vegetables. Allow this to cool a little and skim off as much of the excess fat as possible. Put the beef back in the casserole, surround it with the sautéed vegetables and replace in the oven and cook for 1 hour. Remove beef from casserole to a serving platter, arrange the vegetables round it and if the stock is not the correct consistency, reduce by boiling rapidly.

JP

Beef Stew with Prunes and Pumpkin Scones

Save British beef by eating more of it is what I say. This is a lovely rich comforting stew for the cold winter months. The Pumpkin Scones can be served with the stew or put on top as a cobbler.

900/2lb stewing beef, cubed
25g/1oz dripping
450g/1lb prunes, soaked
1 tbsp flour
300ml/½ pint beef stock

FOR THE MARINADE:
1 bottle red wine
4 tbsp olive oil
1 carrot, sliced
1 onion, sliced
2 cloves garlic, crushed
piece of orange peel
1 tsp juniper berries, crushed
pinch of nutmeg
2 sprigs thyme
2 bayleaves, crushed
6 black peppercorns, crushed
2 tbsp brandy (optional)

PUMPKIN SCONES:
115g/4oz butter, softened
¼ tsp nutmeg
1 tsp salt
freshly ground black pepper
115g/4oz cooked mashed pumpkin
1 egg
120ml/4floz milk
750g/1½lb flour
1 tsp baking powder
milk to glaze

Place the meat in a large non-metallic bowl. Combine all the ingredients for the marinade, pour over the meat and refrigerate for 48 hours, turning occasionally. Strain, reserving the marinade, and wipe dry.

Brown the meat in the hot dripping. Transfer to a casserole and pour over the marinade. Cover and cook in a preheated oven at 150°C/300°F/Gas 2 for 2½ hours. Simmer the soaked prunes in a little salt water for 20–30 minutes or until soft. When the meat has finished cooking, remove from the oven and put on one side. Heat the oven to 220°C/425°F/Gas 7 for the scones.

To make the scones, combine butter, nutmeg, salt, pepper and pumpkin. Mix in the egg and add the milk, sift in flour and baking powder and mix to a soft dough. Turn onto a floured board and knead lightly. Roll to 2cm/¾ inch thick and cut into rounds using a small cup or pastry cutter. Place on a greased baking tray 1cm/½ inch apart and glaze with milk. Bake in the preheated oven for 15–20 minutes. Cool slightly before serving with the stew.

Reduce the meat's stew juices by rapid boiling. Mix the flour and the stock to a paste and blend into the juices and then push through a sieve with the vegetables. Return the meat and the prunes to the sauce and simmer gently on top of the stove for another 15 minutes.

CDW

Beef in Pastry

This dish is also known as Beef Wellington, and I like to think it was created for the Duke of Wellington after his success at Waterloo. This receipt seems very complicated, I know, but well worth it and you can always buy frozen pastry instead of making it. The pastry case is prepared in two parts: a shortcrust bottom to hold the beef, which avoids the sogginess imparted to flaky pastry by juices from the meat and mushrooms, and a flaky pastry top.

1 fillet of beef, trimmed and tied, about 30cm/12in long
900g/2lb mushrooms, finely chopped
5 shallots, finely sliced
55g/2oz butter
120ml/4fl oz Madeira, port or medium sherry
115g/4oz (4 tablespoons) pâté de foie gras

FOR THE MARINADE:
4 tbsp light olive oil
2 medium carrots, sliced
2 medium onions, sliced
2 sticks celery, sliced
pinch of thyme and sage
1 bay leaf
4 cloves
6 peppercorns
1 tsp salt
250ml/8fl oz dry white vermouth
4 tbsp brandy

FOR THE PASTRY:
425g/15oz plain flour
200g/7oz butter, chilled

To prepare the marinade, heat the oil in a saucepan, add all the vegetables, herbs and spices, cover and cook gently until tender. Place the fillet in a long non-metallic dish or casserole, sprinkle with the salt, cover with the vegetable mixture, and pour on the vermouth and brandy. Cover and leave in a cool place or a refrigerator for 24 hours, turning and basting every few hours.

Meanwhile blend the pastry ingredients (except the softened butter) together and chill for 2 hours before using. Butter the outside of a 30x6cm/12x 3in loaf tin. Roll three fifths of the pastry into a rectangle of 41x18cm/16x7in, lay it over the upside-down tin and press into place. Trim so that the pastry forms a case of 3cm/1½in deep. Prick all over with a fork and chill for 30 minutes. Bake in the middle of a preheated oven at 220°C/425°F/Gas 7 until light brown, about 12–15 minutes. Cool for 10 minutes on the tin, then carefully unmould.

Scrape the marinade off the meat, reserve it for the sauce, and dry with kitchen paper. Rub the meat with oil and put in a roasting pan, cover with oiled foil and place in a preheated oven at 220°C/425°F/Gas 7. Roast for 25 minutes, turning and basting halfway through the cooking time. Remove from oven and cool for 30 minutes.

Sauté the mushrooms and shallots in the butter for about 8 minutes, add the Madeira and boil rapidly until all the liquid has evaporated. Stir in 4 tablespoons of pâté, mix well, turn into a bowl and cover until needed.

55g/2oz Cookeen
2tsp salt
175g/6fl oz water, chilled
85g/3oz butter, softened
1 egg, for glazing

FOR THE SAUCE:
2 tsp mushroom ketchup
475ml/16fl oz beef stock
1tbsp tomato purée
1 tbsp cornflour
85ml/3fl oz Madeira, port or sherry
salt and freshly ground pepper

Roll the remaining pastry into a 41x18cm/16x7in rectangle. Over the bottom spread half the softened butter, fold in half to enclose butter. Repeat with the remaining butter and fold again. Roll into a rectangle, then fold in thirds like a business letter. Chill for 2 hours, then roll into another rectangle of 41x25cm/16x10in.

Place the baked bottom case on a buttered baking sheet, spread half the sautéed mushroom mixture on the bottom of the case. Remove the string from the beef, place it on top of the mushrooms and cover with the rest. Beat the egg with half a teaspoon of water and paint the sides of the case, press together and trim if necessary. Paint with the egg glaze. Make cross-hatch marks over the pastry and three vent holes 7.5cm/3in apart. Insert in these tiny foil funnels for escaping steam. Bake in the middle of a preheated oven at 220°C/425°F/Gas 7, for 20 minutes then lower the heat to 190°C/375°F/Gas 5, for another 20 minutes before serving.

To make the sauce, simmer the marinade with the mushroom ketchup in the beef stock and tomato purée for 1 hour. When reduced to 475ml/16fl oz, strain, return to saucepan, and thicken with cornflour mixed with the Madeira, port or sherry. Simmer until shiny and thickened, season to taste.

JP

Beef and Mushroom Croquettes with Sherry

Croquettes were commonplace when I was young as a way of using up the Sunday joint, cold with bubble and squeak for washday Monday and croquettes on Tuesday. They have fallen from fashion but I still love them. This is a particularly tasty recipe and the sherry gives it a fine lift.

55g/2oz mushrooms
350g/12oz cooked beef
20g/¾oz butter
2 tbsp sherry
parsley, finely chopped
salt and freshly ground pepper
flour
dry breadcrumbs

FOR THE WHITE SAUCE:
2 tsp flour
2 tsp butter
150ml/¼ pint milk

For the sauce, make a roux with the butter and flour and slowly blend in the milk. Simmer over a gentle heat until thickened. Wash, trim and chop the mushrooms. Finely chop the leftover beef. Heat the butter in a frying pan and sauté the mushrooms for 1 minute. Add the beef and sherry and season well. Cover and cook over a low flame for 5–10 minutes. Combine with the white sauce and parsley and allow to cool. The mixture should be well seasoned and very thick. Chill the mixture and divide into croquettes the size of small potatoes. Roll in the flour and then in the breadcrumbs. Fry in deep fat until golden brown. Serve with a tomato sauce or a mushroom and sherry sauce.

CDW

Carpet Bag Steak

This is not really a carpet bag steak, it's a carpet bag roast. Redolent of an older age, maybe Dickensian, when huge steaks were eaten by gentlemen in their pubs and clubs. Curiously enough the oysters impart a very good flavour to the beef but do tell any guests in case they are allergic to the mollusc.

1.75kg/4lb piece of topside beef
55g/2oz butter
12–18 oysters, shelled
115g/4oz mushrooms, sliced
150g/6oz breadcrumbs
grated rind of a lemon
1 tbsp parsley
salt and paprika, to taste
1 egg, beaten

Ask the butcher to make a pocket in the topside.

Heat the butter in a frying pan, add the oysters and mushrooms and cook for about 5 minutes. Transfer to a basin, add the breadcrumbs, lemon rind, parsley, seasoning and beaten egg and mix thoroughly. Stuff the mixture into the pocket of the beef and skewer or sew the edges together. Roast in a preheated moderate oven 160°C/325°F/Gas 3 for 2 hours.

JP

Pickled Beef with Soda Scones

At the Uphala festival in the Shetlands this is traditionally served. I like to think of the Scots islanders carrying it as portable fare on their galleys and even the Norse Vikings before them. Once you have pickled your beef there are so many ways you can use it (see Boiled Beef with Lentils and Fennel opposite). This amount of beef will serve 8-10.

1.5kg/3lb brisket or silverside
225g/8oz coarse salt
55g/2oz brown sugar
55g/2 oz black treacle
225g/8oz carrots, sliced
55g/2oz onion, finely chopped

FOR THE SPICE AND HERB MIX:
(this mix of herbs and spices will need to be replenished several times during the process)
½ tsp allspice
½ tsp ground cloves
½ tsp nutmeg
pinch of thyme
black pepper, coarsely crushed
1 crushed bayleaf
1 tbsp saltpetre

FOR THE SCONES:
450g/1lb plain flour
2 tsp bicarbonate of soda
2 tsp cream of tartar
1 tsp salt
85g/3oz lard
300ml/½ pint buttermilk, or sour milk

Have the meat boned and trimmed but not rolled, rub well with the salt and leave overnight. Prepare the herb and spice mixture. Remove the beef from the salt and wipe dry, rub the meat thoroughly with the spice mixture and leave covered in a cool place for 2 days.

Pour the warmed treacle over the meat and spread carefully, then rub the spices into the meat every day for a week.

At the end of the week, roll the spiced beef up and tie firmly with string. Put in a pan of boiling water with the carrots and onions. Simmer gently for 3 hours. If eating cold leave the meat to cool in the liquid.

To make the soda scones, sift the flour with the bicarbonate of soda, tartar and salt. Rub in the lard to a crumbly mixture, pour in the milk stirring with a knife until the mixture is smooth. Shape into 5cm/2in rounds about 1cm/½in thick, set on greased baking sheets and bake at 220°C/425°F/Gas 7 for 8-10 minutes until risen and golden.

CDW

Boiled Beef with Lentils and Fennel

A delicious way of using pickled beef. The fennel's aniseed flavour goes particularly well with the brisket and you can make the lentils as spicy as you wish.

1.5kg/3lb brisket or silverside, see page 80 for preparation
450g/1lb brown lentils
3 tbsp ghee or clarified butter
2 onions, chopped
2.5cm/1in piece of fresh ginger, finely chopped or ¼ tsp powdered ginger
1 tsp turmeric
1 chilli, finely chopped
1.2 litres/2 pints water
juice of ½ a lemon
2–4 (450g/1lb) fennel heads
3 tbsp olive oil
salt and freshly ground pepper

Soak the lentils according to their instructions. Drain well. Melt the ghee in a saucepan and fry the onions and the ginger. Add the lentils, mix in the turmeric and chilli. Add the water, bring to the boil and simmer covered for 15–20 minutes (adding more water if necessary) until the lentils are tender. Drain off any excess liquid, add a squeeze of lemon and season to taste.

Trim the fennel and cut in half. Put in a sealed pan with the oil, salt and pepper, cover tightly and cook over a medium flame for 10–15 minutes until tender. Cut the fennel in half again and add to the lentils. Slice the beef and serve on a bed of vegetables.

CDW

Lamb Kebabs with Spiced Aubergine Sauce

If you are a barbecue addict this makes a change from charred raw sausages and salmonella. Just serve the aubergine sauce as a dip.

900g/2lb lamb, cut into bite-size pieces
4 large tomatoes, cut into quarters
12 medium-sized mushrooms, stalks removed, halved
1 yellow pepper, de-seeded and cut into strips

FOR THE MARINADE:
½ cup olive oil
juice of 1 lemon
1 clove of garlic, finely chopped
1 large onion, finely chopped
1 tsp cumin
½ tsp coriander
½ tsp salt
½ tsp ground black pepper

FOR THE AUBERGINE SAUCE:
900g/2lb aubergine
3 tbsp olive oil
2 cloves of garlic, chopped
1 tsp cumin
pinch of nutmeg
pinch of salt and freshly ground black pepper
juice of 1 lemon
1 tbsp chopped parsley

Combine the marinade ingredients. Marinate the lamb, tomatoes, mushrooms and yellow pepper for 2 hours or overnight. Skewer alternately lamb, tomatoes, mushrooms and yellow pepper.

Slice the aubergines, place in a pie dish and pour over the olive oil, sprinkle on the garlic, cumin, nutmeg, salt, pepper and lemon juice. Cook in a preheated hot oven at 200°C/400°F/Gas 6 for about 30 minutes. Remove from the oven and allow to cool, remove all the black skin and squeeze and discard the bitter juices out of the aubergines. Purée the flesh with the residue and pour into a saucepan.

Grill the kebabs, turning frequently. Heat the aubergine sauce, mix in the chopped parsley. Serve the sauce with the cooked kebabs.

JP

Lamb in Filo Pastry

These dear little chops in their filo pastry could be described as a derivation from the ancient mutton pies but are far more delicate. I would implore you to make sure that they are nice and pink inside – do not overcook.

4x225g/8oz lamb chops, boned
150g/6oz butter
1 tbsp vegetable oil
1 medium onion, chopped
2 cloves of garlic, crushed
225g/8oz mushrooms
1 tbsp chopped parsley
1 tbsp chopped mint
½ tbsp chopped chives
pinch of thyme
juice of 1 lemon
salt and freshly ground pepper
8 tbsp white bread crumbs
12 sheets of filo pastry

Heat the oil and 115g/4oz butter in a frying pan, add the chopped onions and garlic, fry for a couple of minutes, then add the mushrooms. Cook a little more, add the parsley, mint, chives, thyme, lemon juice, seasoning and breadcrumbs and fry until the crumbs begin to brown. Remove from pan and set aside. Put the chops into the frying pan and sear both sides.

Take 3x20cm/8in sheets of filo pastry (if they are bigger there is too much overlap). Cover the rest with a damp cloth to prevent drying out. Melt the remaining butter. Brush each sheet with melted butter, before covering with the next one. When you have buttered 3 sheets, place a lamb chop in the centre, add a quarter of the stuffing and fold the filo pastry over to make a parcel. Repeat with the other lamb chops. (When you are making the parcels make sure that the ones you have done are covered with a damp cloth to prevent the filo from drying out.)

Put the parcels on a baking dish and cook them in a preheated oven at 200°C/400°F/Gas 6 for 20 minutes, reduce heat to 180°C/350°F/Gas 4 and cook for a further 40 minutes.

JP

Artichoke Stuffed Lamb with Honey Tomato Sauce

There is an ancient Roman flavour about this method of serving lamb. The artichokes go very well with it, and while I know the tomatoes are post-Columbian the honey, vinegar and the onions keep the Epicurean theme.

1.75kg/4lb boned leg of lamb
10 artichoke bottoms, chopped
1 onion, chopped
1 tbsp thyme
salt and freshly ground pepper

FOR THE SAUCE:
8 tomatoes, peeled, de-seeded and chopped
1 onion, finely chopped
2 tbsp honey
2 tbsp olive oil
1 tbsp red wine vinegar

Preheat the oven to 180°C/350°F/Gas 4. Mix together the artichokes, onion and thyme. Spread out the piece of lamb, put the mixture on it, roll up the meat and tie it securely. Roast for 1½ hours, or until cooked through.

Simmer the tomatoes and onion with the honey, oil and vinegar for 15 minutes. Purée the mixture, season and add skimmed cooking juices from the lamb. Serve with the meat.

CDW

Harrira

This middle eastern, somewhat peasant, stew is a useful and comforting supper dish which is also good for using up the leftovers from a leg of lamb instead of buying fresh meat should you so desire. Waste not want not.

115g/4oz chickpeas
350/¾ lb lamb, cubed into bite-size pieces
1 large onion, chopped
1 tbsp olive oil
25g/1oz butter
1 tsp ground ginger
1 tsp coriander
1 tsp turmeric
¼ tsp cayenne
¼ tsp cinnamon
salt and freshly ground pepper
900ml–1.2 litres/1½–2 pints chicken stock
400g/14oz chopped, or tinned, tomatoes
55g/2oz long grain rice
pinch of saffron
1 red pepper, skinned, de-seeded and cut in strips
juice of 1 lemon
1 tbsp chopped parsley

Soak the chickpeas overnight, drain and cook rapidly for 10 minutes and then simmer for a further 20 minutes and then drain. Fry the onion in oil and butter until translucent, add the cubed lamb and brown evenly. Add the ginger, coriander, turmeric, cayenne, cinnamon, salt and pepper to taste and fry for a few minutes.

Transfer to a saucepan in which you have the chicken stock, cover and cook gently for an hour. Add the chick peas, tomatoes, rice, red pepper and lemon juice, and cook for a further 30 minutes. Sprinkle with chopped parsley before serving.

JP

Kelp Wrapped Lamb with Pickled Herring

This is an old Northumbrian dish which always amazes people when they find what the stuffing is. You won't believe me until you try it, but it is delicious so please do. The kelp is quite frankly a bit of a whim and the dish is just as good without it!

1 leg of lamb, main bone removed
salt and freshly ground pepper
6 sprigs of thyme
1 onion
6 roll mops
2 tbsp breadcrumbs
large frond of kelp, use tin foil if not available

Pierce the outer skin of the lamb, rub well with salt and pepper and insert the sprigs of thyme. Chop together the onion and herrings and mix with the breadcrumbs and season well. Stuff into the cavity in the lamb. Wrap the lamb well in the kelp or the foil. Roast the lamb in a preheated oven at 180°C/350°F/Gas 4 for 20 minutes per pound.

CDW

Leg of Lamb with Chicken Liver Stuffing

A curious combination you may think, but fear not, a delight awaits all fearless culinary Trojans who are willing to embrace this slightly different receipt. The flavours are divine and the palate will be well rewarded.

1.75kg/4lb leg of lamb, boned
115g/4oz chicken livers
1 medium onion, finely chopped
2 cloves of garlic, crushed
2 tbsp de-fibred and finely chopped celery
1 tbsp chopped parsley
1 tbsp chopped chives
55g/2oz cooked rice
55g/2oz butter
salt and freshly ground black pepper

Ask the butcher to remove the bone, making sure that he leaves a cavity for the stuffing. Melt the butter in a frying pan, fry the livers, lightly sealing them, chop them fairly small, remove and reserve. In the same pan, fry the onions, garlic and celery until the onions are translucent. Add to the livers, with the parsley, chives, cooked rice, salt and black pepper and mix thoroughly. Put the stuffing in the cavity of the leg, cover the opening with either greaseproof paper or tin foil, skewer or sew the other end with string and place the meat in the roasting tin, paper or tin foil side down. Put in a preheated oven at 180°C/350°F/Gas 4 to cook for 2 hours, basting the meat occasionally.

JP

Lamb Casserole with Mint and Chickpeas

I can't remember where I found this Afghani recipe, designed for breast of lamb, but it has a good flavour. My friend Christine said she knew I could really cook when I used up the breasts of lamb in her freezer. I like the cut but it is fiddly, so you can use leg instead.

900g/2lb boned leg or breast of lamb cut into pieces
225g/8oz chickpeas
120ml/4fl oz olive oil
2 onions, finely sliced
600ml/1 pint water
mint leaves
paprika
½ tsp turmeric
salt and freshly ground pepper
450g/1lb peeled potatoes, in large pieces
juice of ½ a lemon

TO SERVE:
yoghurt
finely chopped onion

Soak the chickpeas for 12 hours, then drain. Heat the oil in a large pan and brown the pieces of lamb, add the onions and soften but do not allow to colour. Add the chickpeas and water, bring to the boil and skim well. Stir in the mint, paprika, turmeric, salt and pepper. Cover and simmer for 1 hour. Add the potatoes and the lemon juice and more water if necessary, and cook for 30 minutes or until the potatoes are tender. Serve with yoghurt to which you have added some finely chopped onion.

CDW

Ham with Pea Sauce

I love the combination of ham and peas. Be very careful when cooking your ham to ensure that the bubbles do not break the surface while it is simmering or the meat will toughen. My late brother and I spent many happy and inebriated hours watching our ham. I only hope someone cooks the ham for my funeral as painstakingly and lovingly as I did for his.

900g–1.5kg/2–3lb piece of ham or gammon, with rind removed
600ml/1 pint vegetable stock
300ml/½ pint white wine
2 potatoes, peeled and cubed
1 carrot, cubed
1 parsnip, peeled and cubed
1 onion, finely chopped
150ml/¼ pint sour cream
450g/1lb fresh peas or small packet frozen peas
salt and freshly ground pepper
1 tbsp butter

Simmer the ham in the stock and white wine for 40–60 minutes (allow 20 minutes per pound). Top up with water if the ham is not completely covered. Remove from the stock and keep warm. Cook the vegetables in the stock for about 5 minutes, strain and remove from the pan. Boil the stock fiercely to reduce to about 175ml/6fl oz (about half). Add sour cream and peas and heat through. Purée in a blender, or sieve and season. Reheat the sauce gently, do not let it come to the boil. Sauté the drained root vegetables in a little butter. Slice the meat thinly and serve with vegetables and sauce.

CDW

Pork Fillet with Celery Stuffing

I adore juniper berries and they certainly add zing to this delicious receipt for porky-worky.

2 pork fillets
115g/4oz butter
1 medium onion, finely chopped
2 cloves of garlic, finely chopped
115g/4oz celery, de-fibred and chopped
115g/4oz fresh white breadcrumbs
2 tbsp chopped parsley
½ tsp chopped fresh sage
¼ tsp chopped fresh rosemary
6 juniper berries, crushed
1 egg, lightly beaten
salt and freshly ground pepper
1 tbsp olive oil
300ml/½ pint chicken stock
150/¼ pint white wine
1 tsp grated zest of lemon
beurre manié

Remove fat and sinew from fillets. Cut three quarters through lengthwise, open out, cover with wrapping film or greaseproof paper and flatten the fillets to about 5mm/¼in thick. Melt 55g/2oz butter in a saucepan and add onion, garlic and celery and cook gently until softened but not brown. Add remaining ingredients and bind with beaten egg and season with salt and pepper. Spread the stuffing on the two flattened fillets, roll them up and tie securely with string. Melt 25g/1oz butter and olive oil in the frying pan and brown the fillets. Butter a casserole with remaining butter, add the fillets and cook in a preheated oven at 200°C/400°F/Gas 6 for 40 minutes. Set the fillets aside and keep warm. Add the chicken stock and wine to the casserole and transfer the liquid to the saucepan, bring the liquid to the boil and then thicken with the beurre manié. Slice the pork fillets diagonally and moisten with a little of the sauce. Transfer the remainder of the sauce to the boat.

JP

Pork with Clams

That well-known dish that children love – Pork with Clams! As cooked for the Cotswold Hunt Pony Club, who relished the Portuguese import.

750g/1½lb pork loin
4 cloves of garlic
2 tsp salt
2 tbsp chilli sauce
4 tbsp lard
900g/2lb clams

Mix garlic and salt and crush into a paste. Brush the meat with the paste, then chilli sauce, cover and refrigerate for 24 hours. Cut the meat into squares. Wash the clams thoroughly in several changes of water. Fry the meat in the lard for 10 minutes, or until brown. Add the clams and cook over a high heat so they open quickly, discard any that do not open. Serve at once.

CDW

Illustrated overleaf

Pork Chops Marinated in Yoghurt and Dill

I bought the carcasses of a couple of two-year-old organically raised Tamworth pigs. They were the size of the sides of Highland beef they were hanging next to in my butchers and quite delicious. But it means I have been collecting a few pork recipes. This is a good and easy way of doing chops.

4 pork chops
2 tbsp chilli sauce
225g/8oz Greek yoghurt
3 tbsp chopped dill
oil
salt
coarsely crushed peppercorns

Mix the chilli, yoghurt and dill together, spread over the pork chops and place in a plastic bag. Leave to marinate for 3–24 hours. Remove the chops from the marinade and pat dry. Brush with oil, sprinkle with salt and the crushed peppercorns and cook either under the grill or on a griddle. I gently heat the marinade and serve it with the chops.

CDW

Veal Escalopes with Spinach Stuffing

This is a very pretty dish and the mixture of spinach, rice and vegetables is a great help to this really rather tasteless meat. If you can't get veal or have strong feelings towards little calves then a pork fillet or turkey breast make a very nice escalope.

4 thin veal escalopes
1 medium onion, finely chopped
1 clove of garlic, finely chopped
85g/3oz of butter
1 tbsp vegetable oil
225g/8oz mushrooms, sliced
150g/6oz cooked spinach (weight after cooking)
¾ cup cooked rice
¼ tsp dried oregano
1 tbsp chopped parsley
½ tbsp chopped chives
salt and freshly ground black pepper
300ml/½ pint chicken stock

Soften the onion and garlic in 25g/1oz of butter and ½ tablespoon of oil, add the sliced mushrooms and cook together for a few minutes, stirring often. Squeeze any excess water from the spinach, chop it and add to the mushroom mixture, with the rice, herbs, and seasoning. Mix well. Spread the escalopes with stuffing, roll up and tie with string or secure with small skewers.

Melt the remaining butter and oil in the frying pan and brown the escalope rolls. Put the rolls in an ovenproof dish, add the chicken stock and cook for 45 minutes in a preheated moderate oven at 160°C/325°F/Gas 3.

JP

Stockbridge Marinated Venison

My friend Isabel Rutherford goes off every year to Skye. She stalks and, in her gum boots, climbs mountains that would challenge Sir Edmund Hilary. She returns with a battered ten-year-old stag, which even hounds might disdain, and serves it up chargrilled and tender as best fillet. I have wrung out of her the secret, although she is frightfully airy about this magic trick which even Escoffier might envy.

a large piece of venison (allow 150g/6oz of meat per person)
rind of 1 orange
juniper berries
allspice
a bottle of ordinary claret
a bottle of olive oil
salt and freshly ground pepper
redcurrant jelly

Take your venison and painstakingly cut away all the 'knicker elastic' (Isabel's phrase), put this in a large pot with the orange rind and spices and water and simmer away to form a good stock. If you have an Aga leave the stock in the cool oven for 2 days to form a lovely jelly. Cut the remaining meat into fillets and marinate them in an ocean of claret for 24 hours. Remove them, reserving the wine, pat them dry and cover with olive oil. Add the wine to the stock pot. Leave the venison in the olive oil for another 24 hours. Remove, season and cook on a very hot griddle for a couple of minutes each side. Leave to rest in a warm place for a few minutes and serve with gravy made from your stock pot.

CDW

Venison Pasty

This is a good robust pasty, very medieval and, indeed, along with the pastry trimmings it used to be decorated with hounds and deer. Venison is a curious meat, very lean and so very easy to dry out and, when wild, too gamey for a lot of palates. Certain areas of the country (usually around the old royal hunting forests) will not touch it, which is, no doubt, a genetic legacy of the horrendous Norman game laws.

SERVES 6–8

900g/2lb venison, neck, breast, flank or shoulder
55g/2oz seasoned flour
55g/2oz butter
150ml/¼ pint port
juice of half a lemon
300ml/½ pint venison stock
nutmeg
thyme
salt and freshly ground pepper
175g/6oz butter
550g/1¼lb short crust or rough puff pastry
1 egg, beaten

Cut the venison into small steaks and dust with seasoned flour. Heat a little butter in a frying pan and seal the steaks quickly. Put the meat into a 1.75-2.25 litres/3–4 pint pie dish, add the port, lemon juice and stock, sprinkle with grated nutmeg and thyme, salt and pepper. Lay the butter on top (traditionally it would have been lamb suet), cover with the pastry and glaze with beaten egg. Bake in a preheated oven at 220°C/425°F/Gas 7 for 15 minutes, then at 180°C/350°F/Gas 4 for 1¾ hours.

CDW

Tripe and Onions

I know many people who are passionate about tripe, Clarissa included, but it is the one bit of offal that I have never come to terms with and I have tried it in every possible way. Tripe afficionados, for whom I have cooked this, assure me that it is a fine receipt.

450g/1lb tripe
bouquet garni
2 medium onions, sliced
salt and freshly ground pepper
55g/2oz butter
55g/2oz flour
300ml/½ pint milk
1 tbsp chopped parsley

Cut the tripe into strips about 5cm/2in x 1cm/½in. Tripe is usually partly cooked by the butcher and you will need to cook it again. Place it in a saucepan, add 300ml/½ pint water and bring to the boil for about 1 minute. Discard the water add the same amount of fresh water and the bouquet garni and simmer for about 1½ hours. Check to see that it is very tender. Add the onions to the pan and simmer for another 30 minutes. Season to taste.

Melt the butter in a pan, add the flour and stir with a wooden spoon, do not allow it to brown. Add the milk gradually, stirring continuously. Strain the liquid from the tripe saucepan, discarding the bouquet garni, and add it to the thickened sauce. Sprinkle in the parsley. Put the tripe and onions into a serving dish and pour the parsley sauce over it.

JP

Penis Stew

This unusual stew was sent to me by Joan Saunders and her twin sister, but originates from Marcelle Thomal whose grandfather was an orthodox Russian rabbi. His grandmother's cookery books have been handed down to him and, as he remarked, this receipt makes a change from insect ones. Not for the squeamish.

450g/1lb of penis, ram's or bull's
3 tbsp oil
1 onion, chopped
2 cloves of garlic, peeled and chopped
1 tsp coriander seeds, crushed
1 large tomato, chopped
freshly ground black pepper
1 tsp cumin seeds, crushed
1 tsp salt

Scald the penis, drain and clean it. Place in a saucepan, cover with cold water, bring to the boil, remove any scum and simmer for 10 minutes. Drain and slice. Heat the oil in a large frying pan, add the onion, garlic and coriander and fry until the onion is golden. Add the penis slices and fry on both sides for a few minutes. Stir in the remaining ingredients with a good grinding of pepper, add enough water to cover and bring to the boil. Lower the heat, cover and simmer for about 2 hours or until tender. Add a little water from time to time if necessary to prevent burning.

JP

POULTRY AND GAME

Aliens on motorbikes? No, Clarissa and Jennifer dressed up

for beekeeping

One of the great mysteries of life is why so many people refuse to eat beef because of the BSE scare, which at worst (if you believe it and if you eat cheap beef) promises a one in six million risk, and prefer to eat chicken, which carries a high risk of salmonella. 'Oh,' you may say 'but I buy those free range chicken the supermarkets offer'. However although these may taste better, the problem lies with the modern breeds, the speed with which they are raised and what they are fed on.Five weeks from egg to table is a terrifying thought and the flesh is loose on the bones, allowing disease to proliferate. The reason

free range chickens taste better rests in what they are fed, although they do not have much time to acquire any real flavour. The answer is to buy organically-produced chickens of old breeds: then and only then will you know what chicken should taste like. However, such chickens are more expensive and although they go a lot further, they are hard to get hold of. The answer is to use your chicken as a base for other flavours. The recipe for Mochrum Pie, for instance, has an unusual use of apple with chicken.

Other poultry is a different matter. Ducks and geese are not raised on such a large commercial

'I'm ready for my close up, Mr de Mille.'

scale so they tend to be better reared and have more flavour. Turkey, of course, is a breed apart. Even the most organically reared Bronze has not got a lot of flavour and the commercial ones have none at all. I suspect we only eat turkey for reasons of ritual and religion and certainly if I weren't a food writer I wouldn't touch it from one year's end to the next.

What I really like is the game in this chapter. I love all game and thank heavens the hunting laws, our legacy from William the Conqueror, ensure that it is still seasonal. Rabbit is the odd one out; don't buy imported rabbit, it's inferior and in any event we have far too many of our own. Mine is shot for me by my young friend Sam Scott, but if you don't have access to such a hero, a good butcher will supply you.

If you live in a shooting area or with someone who shoots you will know all about a glut of game. When I worked on a pheasant farm we were endlessly looking for new ways to cook the ruddy things, yet I still love pheasant even after all that over-exposure.

What ever poultry you buy try to buy the best flavour and remember that although a proper organically raised chicken may be more expensive, it will go a lot further. When buying game go to a proper butcher, and remember that a young bird's beak and feet are relatively soft and pliable whilst horney old claws are a sign to casserole the creature or put it in a pie. Game needs to be hung: even if you don't like a very strong flavour you must allow it to hang a while or it will be tough and tasteless.

Collecting the honey at Wandlebury Ring with Bob Lemon, the beekeeper

Maria's Spanish Chicken Andalouse

Serve this fragrant dish with some good plain boiled rice of the long grain variety. This makes a very good summer dish with a fine mixed salad on the side, some crusty bread and a strong red wine such as Rioja.

1.5–1.75kg/3–4lb chicken, jointed
4 tbsp olive oil
55g/2oz butter
16 button onions
2 tsp sugar
225g/8oz mushrooms, sliced
2 cloves of garlic, crushed
1 bouquet garni
750g/1½lb tomatoes, skinned, de-seeded and chopped
1 tbsp tomato purée
3 tbsp chicken stock or water
1 tsp wine vinegar
½ tsp oregano
600ml/1 pint white wine
salt and freshly ground pepper
12 black olives
10 basil leaves, shredded

Sauté the chicken joints in the olive oil until nicely coloured, remove to a casserole. In a separate pan melt the butter, lightly glaze the button onions and add the sugar. Put the sliced mushrooms, button onions, crushed garlic and bouquet garni in the casserole. Mix the tomatoes, tomato purée, chicken stock or water, wine vinegar, wine and oregano. Bring to the boil and simmer for 10 minutes, stirring occasionally. Pour the mixture over the chicken in the casserole, add seasoning and cook in a preheated moderate oven at 190°C/375°F/Gas 5 for 50–60 minutes. Stir in the olives and sprinkle the shredded basil leaves over the chicken before serving.

JP

Chicken with Cockle Sauce

I was doing a cookery demonstration in Dumfries, a part of Scotland separated from Cumbria only by the Solway Firth. During the book signing afterwards I started talking to a most interesting woman who told me that in her part of Britain they cooked chicken with cockles. I tracked down the recipe and can recommend it to you.

2 pints cockles, well washed
1 boiling fowl or large free range hen
1 onion, roughly chopped
1 stick celery, chopped
salt and freshly ground pepper
2 egg yolks
2 tbsp double cream
300ml/½ pint dry white wine
pinch of mace
pinch of cayenne pepper

Open the cockles by simmering in a little salt water and remove from their shells reserving the juice. Truss the fowl and fill the body cavity with two thirds of the cockles, the onion and the celery, and season well. Cook in a chicken brick or in an earthenware jar set in boiling water on top of the stove, for about 2 hours or until tender. If you have neither a brick nor a jar handy, wrap the bird tightly in several layers of tin foil, put in a roasting tin half full of water and cook in the oven at 180°C/350°F/Gas 4. Remove the fowl and thicken the gravy with the blended egg yolks and cream, add the remaining cockles, juice and wine, season and add the mace and cayenne.

Carve the bird and pour over the sauce.

CDW

Wylde Green Chicken

Commonly known as Wild Green Chicken. This is a dish I invented when staying with Christine, my best friend from school, who lives in Wylde Green Road in Birmingham. It is a dish designed to deal with the problem of tasteless chicken, and it proved so popular with my godchildren that I had to write it down.

6 chicken breasts
2 tbsp crunchy peanut butter
2 cloves of garlic, finely chopped
2 tbsp olive oil
1 tsp dried mustard
1 tsp paprika
1 tsp each salt and freshly ground pepper
1 tsp chilli sauce
1 tbsp dark rum or wine vinegar
300ml/½ pint water

Mix together the peanut butter, garlic and half the oil. Lay the chicken breasts in a dish, pour the mixture over them, turn and work well into the meat. Leave to stand for at least 30 minutes. In a large frying pan heat the rest of the oil and dissolve the mustard, paprika, salt and pepper into it. Tip the chicken breasts with the marinade into the pan and sauté until they are coloured. At this stage I usually cut them into pieces in the pan. Add the chilli sauce, the rum and the water and cook over a low heat until they are cooked through, usually about 10 minutes. Serve with new potatoes or rice and a green salad.

CDW

Chicken Simla

Shades of the British memsahibs reclining in Simla. If you prefer, use a good curry paste which you can buy either hot or medium according to your taste. Though not a true Indian receipt this is surprisingly good and can be eaten either hot or cold.

1.5kg/3lb chicken jointed
85g/3oz butter
1 medium onion, chopped
1 stick celery, chopped into
2.5cm/1in pieces
1 sprig parsley
1 sprig fresh thyme
1 bayleaf
salt and freshly ground pepper
1 clove of garlic, crushed
2 tsp curry powder
pinch of saffron
300ml/½ pint Bechamel sauce
120ml/¼ pint coconut milk
120ml/¼ pint single cream
juice of 1 lemon

Melt the butter and gently fry the chicken joints and onion until the joints are a pale golden colour, do not allow to brown. Lay the celery, parsley, thyme and bayleaf in a casserole, place the chicken joints on top and sprinkle over the salt and pepper, crushed garlic, curry powder and cooked onions. Cook in a preheated moderate oven 180°C/350°F/Gas 4 for 35–40 minutes until the chicken is cooked but not brown. Remove the chicken, put it in a clean casserole and replace in the oven to cook for a further 20 minutes while you prepare the sauce.

Infuse the saffron in 2 tablespoons of water.

To the remaining casserole add the Bechamel sauce and coconut milk, mix to take up all the chicken juices and transfer to a saucepan. Bring the sauce to the boil and simmer gently for about 20 minutes – stirring frequently. Strain into another saucepan, add the cream and reheat – you may add a little more coconut milk if the consistency is not quite right. Strain the infused saffron water and add to the sauce with the lemon juice. Pour the sauce over the chicken and serve.

JP

Calcutta Chicken Croquettes

My maternal grandfather died young of the demon drink, leaving my grandmother with two young children. Fortunately she met my step-grandfather, an extremely wealthy Sephardic Jew from Calcutta. For years she refused to marry him because he was a Jew and she was a Catholic. They lived together in great luxury with sixty indoor servants in what is now the British Residency in Singapore. I was reminded of this excellent dish by Claudia Roden's brilliant *Book of Jewish Food* and dug out my step-great grandmother's version.

225g/8 oz cold basmati rice (cook and drain but don't rinse, to leave in the starch)
450g/1lb finely minced chicken
2 onions, finely chopped
5–7.5cm/2–3in piece of ginger, grated
1 tsp garam masala
½ tsp turmeric
1 bunch coriander, finely chopped
1 bunch flat parsley, finely chopped
4 tbsp chicken fat or vegetable oil for frying

In a large bowl mix all the ingredients except the chicken fat or oil. If the rice is not sticky enough you can add an egg to bind. This can be done in a food processor but I feel the resulting mixture doesn't have enough texture. Form into 5cm/2in croquettes and fry in the hot chicken fat or oil until deep gold.

CDW

Oriental Chicken Pudding

This looks magnificent when presented steaming at the table – full of different flavours and good for lunch on a cold winter's day. You could use suet instead of butter in the pastry. Great for hungry boys.

900g/2lb boned chicken breast cut into chunks
25g/1oz plain flour
salt and freshly ground black pepper
olive oil
3 heads chicory
2 tbsp freshly chopped coriander
1 bunch spring onions, chopped
2 large cloves of garlic
coarsely grated rind and juice of 1 lemon
1 tbsp soy sauce
5cm/2in piece of fresh ginger, grated

FOR THE PASTRY:
150g/6oz self-raising flour
3 tsp paprika
1 tsp ground mace
2 tsp paprika
2 tsp chervil
3–4 pinches cayenne pepper
115g/4oz fresh white breadcrumbs
150g/6oz frozen butter
1 egg

Coat the chicken pieces with the plain flour seasoned with salt and pepper. Heat the olive oil in a heavy-bottomed pan over a high heat. Add the chicken pieces and brown on all sides and then leave on one side to cool.

Mix together the self-raising flour, spices, breadcrumbs, chervil, cayenne pepper and salt to taste in a bowl. Hold the butter in a damp cloth at one end and grate it into the mixture, mixing it with your hands. Whisk the egg in a measuring jug and top it up with water to a total of 1.75ml/6fl oz. Gradually mix the liquid into the flour and butter. Bring it together and form a ball. Save a quarter of the dough for a lid. Roll out the rest of the dough fairly thinly into a circle with a diameter of about 35cm/14in. Line a 1.75–litre/3–pint pudding basin with the pastry leaving the edges to overlap the top of the basin. Don't worry if the pastry breaks, just gently patch it together with your hand.

Cut the chicory into thick slices and mix with the coriander, spring onions, garlic, chicken, lemon rind and soy sauce. Add the lemon juice and season. Spoon this mixture into the basin so that it forms a mound at the top. Fold the pastry over the filling and wet the edges. Roll out the saved dough into a circle big enough to form the top. Seal the edges by pressing them lightly. Take a buttered piece of greaseproof paper and make a pleat in the middle before putting it over the top of the pudding. Put a piece of foil loosely over the paper and tie both securely with string. Make a handle with string and lower the pudding into a saucepan of boiling water. Cover and boil gently for 3 hours, check the water level at regular intervals and top up as required.

JP

Chicken with Red Pepper Sauce

It is always useful to have different ways to prepare chicken, fast becoming the staple food in many a household. Do try to get a chicken which has run naked and unencumbered throughout its formative years – otherwise known as free range. It really does make all the difference and the bones make wonderful stock.

1.5kg/3lb chicken, jointed
55g/2oz butter
2 tbsp vegetable oil
6 small shallots
2 red peppers, de-seeded
2 cloves of garlic
150ml/¼ pint white wine
salt and freshly ground pepper
1 tsp dried oregano
1 tbsp tomato purée
1 tbsp chopped parsley

Melt the butter with the vegetable oil and add the shallots, red peppers and garlic. Fry gently until the shallots and pepper are just soft. Remove with a slotted spoon and set aside. Turn up the heat and fry the chicken joints on both sides. Put the chicken joints in a casserole dish, spoon the peppers and shallots on top, pour in the wine, add 1 teaspoon salt and ½ teaspoon pepper and the oregano. Cook in a preheated medium oven at 190°C/375°F/Gas 5 for 45–55 minutes. Remove the chicken joints and pour the liquid with the peppers, shallots and garlic into a liquidiser. Add the parsley and liquidise. Pour the sauce over the chicken joints and serve.

JP

Mochrum Chicken Pie

Flora Stuart, President of the Belted Galloway Society (Belted Galloways are famous beef cattle), served me this recipe, an invention of her butler John. She lives in a romantic fourteenth century castle called Old Place of Mochrum, hence the name. When she served this pie to me I couldn't guess what the topping was just by looking at it, as it has an interesting pale green colour. It is a great pie and just as good cold as hot.

4 cooking apples
3 onions, chopped
55g/2oz butter
salt and freshly ground pepper
225g/8oz shortcrust pastry
450g/1lb cooked chicken meat

Peel, core and chop the apples and cook in a little water until they cook to a purée. Fry the onions in the butter until soft and coloured, season and allow to cool. Line a pie dish with your shortcrust pastry and place your onions in the bottom, place the chicken meat on top and level off. Heap the apple on top of the chicken, mound it slightly and cover with a lattice of pastry. Bake at 220°C/425°F/Gas 7 for 10 minutes, then reduce to 180°C/350°F/Gas 4 for 30 minutes.

CDW

Chicken, Polenta and Quail Egg Pie

This is a very good pie to take cold on a picnic or even lukewarm if you have just cooked it. The five-spice powder gives a hint of China which is a change from Branston pickle.

1.75kg/4lb chicken, jointed
600ml/1 pint chicken stock
300ml/½ pint white wine
1 large onion, sliced
1 bayleaf
10 peppercorns
1 heaped tsp five-spice powder
1½–2 tbsp polenta
55g/2oz butter
juice of 1 lemon
150g/6oz cooked ham lardons
8 quail eggs, hardboiled
salt and freshly ground pepper
225g/½lb shortcrust pastry
beaten egg, to glaze

Put the jointed chicken in a saucepan and cover with the chicken stock and the wine. Add the sliced onion, bayleaf, peppercorns and five-spice powder. Bring to the boil, lower the heat and simmer gently for 45 minutes. Remove from heat, add polenta, lemon juice and butter and stir. Simmer for another 15 minutes or so until you think the chicken is tender. Remove saucepan from heat and allow to cool.

Skin and bone the chicken joints. Place the chicken meat in a large pie-dish, add the cooked ham lardons, the shelled quail eggs and the sauce from the pan. Taste for seasoning and cover with short-crust pastry. A nice glaze is obtained by brushing the pastry with a beaten egg. Cook in a preheated moderate oven at 200°C/400°F/Gas 6 for 25–30 minutes or until golden.

JP

Wild Duck with Sauce Bigerard

Bigarade is the French name for bitter Seville oranges which only have a short season, so grab them when you can during the marmalade-making days. The sauce is most excellent with mallard or wild duck, enriching the rather dry flesh. Otherwise you can serve the sauce with a domestic duck or pieces thereof. The ducks should be served pink inside which takes about 30 minutes in a preheated oven at 180°C/350°F/Gas 4.

2 x 1.75kg/4lb ducks of your choice
1 onion, chopped
1 large carrot, chopped
1 bouquet garni
600ml/1 pint water

FOR THE SAUCE:
2 Seville oranges
25g/1oz butter
1 level tbsp plain flour
250ml/8fl oz chicken or game stock
2 tsp sugar
salt and freshly ground pepper
Madeira or port

Make a stock with the giblets, onion, carrot and bouquet garni. Roast the ducks in a preheated oven at 180°C/350°F/Gas 4 for 20–30 minutes, depending on the degree or rareness you like.

To make the sauce, pare the rind off the oranges very thinly so that no pith is left on the peel. Cut into tiny strips and fling into a pan of boiling water for 5 minutes to blanch. Drain through a sieve and set aside. Melt the butter in a little saucepan, stir in the flour and cook gently until it becomes a pale coffee colour. Add the stock a little at a time, skimming the while to provide a smooth sauce, and simmer for a further 15 minutes. Add the blanched rind and the sugar, season to taste and add the juice from the roasting pan after you have drained off the fat.

If you want to make this sauce when Seville oranges are out of season, cheat by using 1 ordinary orange and a piled tablespoon of bitter marmalade, but omit the sugar.

JP

115

Wild Duck with Barley

There seems to be an attempt to make barley a fashion food item, although one attempt at eating a barley risotto cures most people. However I am very fond of barley properly utilised. Try this curious way of preparing it which comes from a Swedish recipe and which I think goes well with the richness of the duck.

2 wild duck, if possible with their livers
salt and freshly ground pepper
115g/4oz prunes
450ml/¾ pint water
3 apples, chopped
juice of 1 orange
2 tbsp honey
1 tbsp red wine vinegar
2 tbsp oil
115g/4oz barley, cooked
55g/2oz Greek yoghurt
2 tbsp grated horseradish

Rub the outside of the duck with salt and pepper. Stuff with prunes and apples and livers. Smear with soft butter and roast in a very hot oven – 230°C/450°F/Gas 8 – for 20–30 minutes depending on rareness liked, baste during cooking.

In a pan boil together for a few minutes orange juice, honey, vinegar and oil. Stir in the barley and season, add the yoghurt and the horseradish and heat through. When the duck is cooked, make a thin gravy from the juices and the water, carve the duck and serve in the barley with the gravy on the side.

CDW

Duckling with Green Grapes

Green grapes are usually identified with receipts called Veronique, but not in this case. The sweetness of the grapes with the damson jelly goes very well with duckling and cuts the fatty content of the bird. A good dinner party dish when served with a purée of celeriac and potato.

2.25kg/5lb duckling
salt and freshly ground pepper
350g/12oz white seedless grapes
2 tbsp brandy
150ml/¼ pint dry white wine
1 tbsp damson jelly
11 bouquet garni
¼ tsp grated nutmeg
1 tbsp chopped parsley
1 tbsp cornflour

Prick the duck all over, rub salt and pepper on to the skin, put in a roasting tin in a pre-heated oven at 220°C/425°F/Gas 7 for 30 minutes until the duck is light brown. While the duck is cooking, wash and strain grapes, reserve a few for decoration and liquidise the rest. Take the duck out of the oven and reduce the heat to 180°C/350°F/Gas 4.

Heat the brandy, ignite and pour over the duck. Cut the duck into serving portions and put it into a casserole. Discard the fat from the roasting tin. Pour over the wine, grape juice, damson jelly, bouquet garni, nutmeg and parsley. Agitate with a wooden spoon, making sure that you scrape up all the brown bits in the roasting tin. Pour the liquid over the duck portions in the casserole and cook for another 45–60 minutes. Remove joints from casserole, discard bouquet garni and thicken the liquid with the cornflour dissolved in a little water. Add the remaining grapes. Pour some of the sauce over the duck and put the remainder in a sauce boat.

JP

Duck in Red Wine Sauce

This is a useful dish to prepare in advance if you are a working person. Just heat it up before you need to eat it. The flavours intensify, as with many a casserole dish, on reheating.

1.75kg/4lb duck, jointed
salt and freshly ground pepper
25g/1oz plain flour
55g/2oz butter
2 tbsp olive oil
55g/2oz chopped shallots
115g/4oz bacon lardons
300ml/½ pint red wine
6 crushed peppercorns
1 bayleaf
600ml/1 pint chicken stock
16 whole button onions
225g/8oz mushrooms, sliced
1 tsp sugar

FOR THE BEURRE MANIE:
40g/1½ oz butter
25g/1oz flour

Sprinkle duck joints with salt, pepper and flour and sauté in 25g/1oz melted butter and 1 tablespoon of oil until golden brown. Place duck joints in casserole dish. Cook the shallots and lardons in the oil and butter for a few minutes. Add the wine, peppercorns and bayleaf. Boil to reduce to half, then add the stock and again reduce by half. Strain sauce over duck and cook gently in a pre-heated oven at 190°C/375°F/Gas 5, for 1 hour but check to make sure the duck joints are cooked.

Meanwhile melt the remaining butter and oil in the frying pan, add the button onions, sprinkle with sugar and brown. After the duck has been cooking for 30 minutes add the onions and the raw mushrooms. When the duck joints are cooked, set to one side, check the sauce for consistency and seasoning and, if necessary, thicken with the beurre manie. To make this, knead the butter and flour together and form into a small knob.

JP

Grouse Pie

If you have a good game butcher he will sell you old grouse quite cheaply as everyone wants the young birds for roasting. This is a flavoursome robust country pie and the gravy is enriched by the addition of steak. This was a custom which grew in the Georgian age with the greater availability of beef, thanks to the Agricultural Revolution.

a brace of grouse
450g/1lb beef, rump or topside
55g/2oz diced bacon
2 eggs, hardboiled
salt and freshly ground pepper
pinch of mace
pinch of nutmeg
600ml/1 pint game stock
1 tbsp sherry
550g/1¼ lb puff pastry
beaten egg, to glaze

Divide each grouse into four leg and four breast pieces, cut the steak into 2.5cm/1in cubes. Arrange in a 1.75ml/3 pint pie dish and top with the bacon and the hardboiled eggs. Pour on enough stock to cover. Put a lid on the dish, or cover with foil and cook in a preheated oven at 160°C/325°F/Gas 3 for 1½ hours. Remove from oven and turn heat up to 220°C/425°F/Gas 7. Allow dish to cool slightly, add sherry, cover with a lid of the puff pastry and bake for a further 30 minutes. Serve with creamed potatoes and green vegetables.

CDW

Guinea Fowl with Jerusalem Artichokes, Mushrooms and Button Onions

For those who are a little faint of heart and do not like the strong flavour of a well-hung pheasant, this provides an ideal alternative. Guinea fowl can be dry, but this receipt works a treat every time.

1 large plump guinea fowl, or
2 small ones
1 tbsp oil
115g/4oz butter
4 shallots, finely chopped
1 clove of garlic
225g/½lb mushrooms, sliced
450g/1lb Jerusalem artichokes
16 button onions
150ml/¼ pint single cream
2 egg yolks
salt and freshly ground pepper
1 tbsp chopped parsley

Brown the guinea fowl in the oil and half the butter in a large frying pan and put in a casserole. Fry the shallots and garlic and add to the casserole. Cook the guinea fowl in a preheated moderate oven at 190°C/375°F/Gas 5 for 1 hour.

In the meantime, fry the mushrooms gently for 2–3 minutes. Cut the artichokes into fairly uniform pieces. Parboil the button onions and artichokes for no more than 5 minutes and strain. Add the mushrooms, button onions and artichokes to the casserole and cook for a further 30 minutes. Remove casserole from the oven, pour heated sherry over the fowl and ignite. Remove the fowl and joint it, arrange on a serving dish with the vegetables around it and keep it warm.

Stir the cream into the juices remaining in the casserole with a wooden spoon, then pour into a saucepan and boil rapidly to reduce. Remove from the heat and stir in the beaten egg yolks with salt and pepper to taste. Pour a little sauce over the guinea fowl and sprinkle over the chopped parsley. Serve the remainder of the sauce in a sauceboat.

JP

Pheasant with Chestnuts in Pastry

When I worked on the pheasant farm in Sussex I learnt to sympathise with those who have endless pheasants to cook and spent a lot of time thinking up recipes. I particularly like this one because it is so good for a dinner party. You can get to the stage where you wrap the pheasant earlier in the day and just bung it in the oven at the relevant time, and the pastry stops it drying out. It's also a good recipe for guinea fowl and chicken.

1 pheasant
450g/1lb chestnuts
85g/3oz butter
225g/8oz pheasant or chicken livers, chopped
225g/8oz bacon, minced
2 onions, chopped
salt and freshly ground pepper
300ml/½ pint game or chicken stock
350g/12oz puff pastry
1 egg yolk, beaten

FOR THE SHERRY SAUCE:
55g/2oz butter
55g/2oz flour
750ml/1¼ pints chicken stock
salt and pepper
50ml/3tbsp double cream
30g/1oz butter
50ml/3tbsp dry sherry

Peel the chestnuts and simmer in salted water until tender but still whole. Mix together the bacon, livers, chestnuts, onion and 25g/1oz of the butter, and seasoning. Stuff the pheasant with the mixture. Brown the pheasant in the rest of the butter add the stock and roast in a preheated oven at 200°C/400°F/Gas 6 for 20 minutes, turning onto the other side half way through. Baste frequently. Remove from the oven and allow to cool. Roll the pastry out and wrap the bird in it. Cut a slit for steam and brush with the egg yolk. Bake at 180°C/375°F/Gas 5 for 40 minutes.

For the sauce, heat the butter in a heavy pan. Add the flour and cook for 3 minutes stirring continuously. Add the stock to the roux a bit at a time. Whisking continuously reduce the heat and simmer for 30 minutes stirring and skimming every 10 minutes. Add the cream and simmer over a low heat for 10 minutes. Season and pass through a conical sieve into a clean saucepan. Over a low heat, whisk in the butter a little at a time. Remove from the heat, add the sherry and serve with the pheasant.

CDW

Pheasant with Cranberries, Red Wine and Port

I really prefer a traditionally cooked pheasant with all the trimmings. However, if you belong to a sporting family and have a plethora of the birds this makes a welcome change.

2 young pheasants
55g/2oz butter
1 onion
300ml/½ pint chicken stock
300ml/½ pint red wine
1 glass of port (sherry glass)
2 tbsp French mustard
juice of 1 orange
juice of 1 lemon
4 tbsp cranberry sauce
salt and freshly ground pepper

FOR THE BEURRE MANIE:
25g/1oz flour
40g/1½oz butter

Spread 25g/1oz of butter over each bird and put half an onion in each cavity. Roast the pheasants in a preheated moderate oven at 180°C/350°F/Gas 4 for about 1 hour. After 30 minutes baste and turn the pheasants upside down.

Meanwhile add to a saucepan the chicken stock, red wine, port, mustard, orange and lemon juice and cranberry sauce. Bring to the boil and simmer for 20 minutes. For the beurre manie, work together the flour and butter.

Remove the pheasants from the casserole and set aside. Add the juices left in the casserole to the saucepan and while it is simmering thicken it with knobs of beurre manie.

JP

123

Pheasant with Lemon and Capers

I first made this dish at a Red Cross demonstration in Dumfries for Eileen Duncombe. I was somewhat alarmed when I discovered they were going to raffle the food as it was an untried dish. So busy am I these days that I have to invent recipes every time I'm near a stove. However, I'm happy to say this was a success – new pheasant recipes are always welcome.

1 pheasant, cut in strips
zest and juice of 4 lemons
115g/4oz plain flour
salt and freshly ground pepper
4 tbsp oil
1 tbsp capers, roughly chopped
8 tbsp brown sugar
300ml/½ pint game or chicken stock

Marinade the pheasant strips overnight in the lemon juice. Remove meat, reserving the juice, pat dry with kitchen paper and coat with seasoned flour. Brown the strips in the oil in a heavy pan, then add capers, lemon zest and brown sugar, and cook for 2–3 minutes. Heat the stock and lemon juice together and serve as a sauce.

CDW

Cream Smothered Pheasant

For people with an endless supply of the little creatures, another way to enjoy pheasant.

1 large or 2 small pheasants
1 tbsp vegetable oil
85g/3oz butter
1 medium onion
2 cloves of garlic
600ml/1 pint white wine
300ml/½ pint stock, made
from giblets minus liver
bouquet garni of parsley,
bayleaf and thyme
pinch of nutmeg
salt and freshly ground pepper
25g/1oz flour
300ml/½ pint double cream
3 egg yolks, beaten
1 tbsp chopped parsley

Sauté the pheasant in the oil and 55g/2oz butter in a frying pan until golden brown all over. Put the pheasant in a casserole. Fry the onion and garlic in the pan but do not brown. Add the wine, stock, bouquet garni, nutmeg, salt and pepper and bring to the boil, then pour over the pheasant. Cook in a preheated medium oven at 200°C/400°F/Gas 6 until the pheasant is tender, about 1–1½ hours. Transfer the pheasant to the serving dish and keep warm. Boil the casserole juices in a saucepan to reduce by half.

Melt the remaining butter in a saucepan, add the flour, stir and cook for a few minutes. Gradually add the pan juices, stirring constantly, then add the cream. Lower the heat and simmer for a few minutes. Remove the saucepan from the heat and stir in the beaten egg yolks. Test for seasoning and sprinkle with parsley. Pour a little over the pheasant and serve the remainder in a sauceboat.

JP

Rabbit Isabel

My friend Isabel produced this recipe for me from the Borders. I cooked it at the Scone Palace Game Fair, which is a great event of the Scottish year and was originally set up by my friend Henry Crichton-Stuart. When I demonstrated it they presented me with two whole rabbits, which I cut up on stage. It is a fine recipe for using all the rabbit, is delicious and economical.

1 young rabbit per person, fillets and leg meat removed
25g/1oz plain flour
salt and freshly ground pepper
¼ tsp dry mustard
¼ tsp cayenne pepper
1 egg white
1 slice good bacon per two rabbit fillets
sorrel or sage leaves
115g/4oz butter
1 onion, finely chopped
glass of white wine

Make seasoned flour with salt, pepper, dry mustard and cayenne pepper. In a food processor finely mince the leg meat, add the egg white and seasoning and blend to a paste. Flatten the fillets and flour lightly. Lay a piece of bacon cut to fit on one fillet, spread a layer of the mousseline of rabbit and egg white onto the bacon and lay your sorrel or sage leaves on top of this. Place the other rabbit fillet on top to make a parcel.

In a heavy-lidded frying pan melt the butter and gently fry the onion, add the rabbit parcel and brown, turning carefully. Season, pour on white wine, cover and cook gently for 10 minutes turning the parcel halfway through. Check that the rabbit is tender, and serve with garlic-puréed potatoes and a green vegetable.

CDW

Illustrated on previous page

Rabbit with Chocolate

This is a very early Spanish recipe which was presumably brought back from the New World. As they have no rabbits in Mexico or South America I imagine the dish was designed for guinea pig or even chihuahua. However, it works very well with rabbit and has an excellent flavour.

900g–1.5kg/2–3lb rabbit, cut into 8 serving pieces
55g/2oz lard
115g/4oz salt pork, finely diced
25g/1oz plain flour
salt and freshly ground pepper
12 shallots, peeled
½ glass dry red wine
120ml/4fl oz water
1 bayleaf
1 handful parsley, chopped
generous pinch of thyme
55g/2oz blanched almonds
55g/2oz pine nuts
1½ tsp unsweetened plain chocolate, finely grated

In a heavy-based lidded pan melt the lard and fry the pork until crisp and browned. Remove to kitchen paper to drain. Mix together the flour and salt and pepper and coat the rabbit pieces, brown them carefully in the fat in the pan and remove to a plate. Fry the shallots in the fat and remove to the plate with the rabbit. De-glaze the pan with wine and water, return the pork and rabbit, add the bayleaf and herbs. Reduce to a low heat, cover and cook gently for 30 minutes.

Grind the almonds and pine nuts in a blender or pestle and mortar, and mix with the grated chocolate. Add this and the onions to the rabbit, stir thoroughly and add a little more wine if dry. Cover again and cook for a further 30 minutes or until rabbit is tender. Serve at once.

CDW

Baked Rabbit

I know some people won't eat rabbit for various reasons but I wish they would try. The flesh is succulent with a good flavour – it has little or no fat and can only be commended in every way. The wilder the rabbit the better the flavour and you will be doing the farmers a great favour.

1 rabbit, cut up and jointed
25g/1oz plain flour
2 tbsp olive oil
2 thick bacon slices, cubed
1 large onion, thickly sliced
1 large clove of garlic, finely chopped
½ tsp paprika
300ml/½ pint dry white wine
1 tbsp tomato purée
salt and freshly ground pepper
1 bayleaf

FOR THE MARINADE:
1 cup red wine
1 cup red wine vinegar
1 clove of garlic, chopped
2 sticks celery, chopped
sprig of thyme
sprig of parsley

Place the jointed rabbit in the marinade and leave overnight, preferably, or for several hours. Remove the rabbit pieces, dry with kitchen paper and dust lightly with flour. Heat the olive oil in a frying pan and fry the rabbit pieces until light golden brown and place in a casserole.

Sauté the bacon and onion in the frying pan, add the garlic and paprika and cook a little longer. Add wine, tomato purée, salt, pepper and bay leaf, bring to the boil and simmer for about 5 minutes. Pour over the rabbit and cook in a preheated moderate oven at 180°C/350°F/Gas 4 for about 1½ hours or until the rabbit is tender.

CDW

Burnetts Woodcock

My friends Jane and George, to whom this dish is dedicated, are known as the Dona-kebabs because they gave me a sheep for my fiftieth birthday and called it Kebab to guard against sentimentality. George is a keen shot and is always looking for different ways of preparing woodcock. You can use wood pigeon if you are not so fortunate.

4 woodcock, properly hung
115g/4oz butter
1 rasher of bacon per bird

FOR THE POTATO CAKES:
750g/1½lb waxy potatoes
2 egg whites and 1 yolk
1 tbsp capers, chopped
150ml/¼ pint whipping cream
25g/1oz butter

FOR THE SAUCE:
4 pigeon livers (use pheasant or chicken if not available)
55g/2oz butter
small glass white wine
2 tbsp beef stock
10 juniper berries, crushed
salt and freshly ground pepper
squeeze of lemon juice

First make the potato cakes. Boil the potatoes, mash them and let them dry well. Beat the egg whites very stiffly but not dry. Mix the egg yolk and capers and cream into the mash and fold in the egg whites. Form small cakes and fry in the butter until brown.

Spread each woodcock generously with butter and cover with a bacon rasher. Roast in a preheated very hot oven at 220°C/425°F/Gas 7 for 10–15 minutes, depending on how you like them, more if you must.

For the sauce, sauté the livers in butter until just cooked, mash and sieve them. Put the purée in a pan, thin with white wine and stock, add juniper berries, seasoning and lemon juice, and simmer for a few minutes.

Place the cooked woodcock on the potato cakes and serve with the sauce.

CDW

Turkey Pilaff in Filo Pastry

I am not a great fan of turkey but I am always being asked for ways of using it and there is no doubt that if you cook one there will be leftovers. A pilaff is an interesting Persian dish and enclosed in filo pastry this has quite a Turkish flavour, even if the name of the bird is merely a historical mistake.

150g/6oz butter
1 onion, finely chopped
55g/2oz pine nuts
225g/8oz long grain rice
600ml/1 pint chicken stock
2 tomatoes
2 tbsp currants
½ tsp allspice
pinch of nutmeg
½ tsp sugar
½ tsp cayenne
salt and freshly ground pepper
½ red pepper, chopped
1 stick celery, chopped
1 small courgette, chopped
4 chicken livers, chopped
225g/8oz turkey raw or
cooked, sliced in thin strips
juice and rind of 1 lemon
8 sheets filo pastry
melted butter

In a large pan heat 115g/4oz of the butter and cook the onion until soft, add pine nuts and rice and cook over heat until slightly coloured. Add half the chicken stock a little at a time to allow the rice to absorb it. Stir in the tomatoes, currants, spices, sugar and seasoning. Pour on the rest of the chicken stock and bring to the boil, reduce the heat, cover and simmer until the rice is tender and the stock is absorbed, about 15–20 minutes.

In a small pan heat the remaining butter and sauté the pepper, celery and courgette. Add the chicken livers and turkey strips if uncooked, season and cook until the chicken livers are just done. Add this to the rice mixture with lemon juice and rind. Grease an 20cm/8in cake tin. Brush each sheet of filo with melted butter. Place sheets to cover inside of tin, letting them hang over the sides. Fill with the mixture, fold pastry over the top and brush with melted butter. Bake at 180°C/350°F/Gas 4 for 25–30 minutes until golden brown. Turn onto a dish and serve hot or cold.

CDW

SIDE DISHES

Jennifer and Clarissa about to be swept away at Wandlebury Ring by warden of the park Bill Clark

To me the making or breaking of any menu rests with the accompaniments to the main course. It is all very well to have a splendid central dish but so often one sees the cook's concentration wavering when it comes to the vegetables. I am very lucky to have so many friends who grow their own vegetables and give me their surplus, but I have to admit it is very hard to find decent vegetables to buy. I don't know what happens to our own home-grown vegetables, we are told the growers are in thrall to the supermarkets but if you check the shelves they are full of foreign imports, especially the unspeakable Dutch ones. I suppose somewhere in the world people are marvelling at English

carrots or Scots broccoli. Now that I am back in the catering business I see the difficulty even more. I had to go to a supermarket to buy the Jersey Royals I had put on a menu and one day the very helpful girl from Anderson's our veg suppliers told me a particular item had not been good enough from the market so she had gone to Sainsburys for our supplies! Don't think I am weakening on supermarkets, although Jennifer has been known to visit them; their vegetables are irradiated, chilled out of existence and tasteless, and the only thing to do with tasteless products is to use them as a base and add other flavours to them.

When designing your menu, remember that in a piece of jewellery every minor stone plays its part. There is nothing worse than bowls of unadorned vegetables untouched by butter or oil or a sprinkling of parsley or whatever. Restaurants have real problems with this and either serve you a demi-lune salad dish full of uninteresting flaccid sad little objects or increasingly no vegetables at all save a token infant by way of garnish.

Buy the best vegetables you can, if they don't have much taste do something to them until they do and mound your serving bowls high to give a feeling of abundance – if you do have any leftovers, you could always try making some soup with them.

Baked Beetroot with Sour Cream and Mint

I learnt this recipe years ago from one of my greatest friends, Nandy Routh, wife of Jonathan (the original Candid Camera man). Alas she was killed in a motor accident but this splendid vegetable dish, originally Persian I think, always reminds me of her.

raw beetroots
olive oil
salt and freshly ground pepper
sour cream
finely chopped fresh mint or
good dried mint

I find the long triangular beetroots are best for this dish but it really doesn't matter. Place as many of the beets as you deem necessary in a roasting tin or baking tray. Caress them with olive oil and season with salt and pepper. Bake in a preheated oven at 200°C/400°F/Gas 6 for about 1 hour or until tender to the pierce of a sharp knife or skewer. Serve, split open with a good dollop of sour cream and a generous sprinkling of chopped mint.

JP

Gratin of Beetroot

I love beetroot, its wonderful medieval colour cheering us in the grey months, its texture and sweetness, and the way it lends itself so well to pickles and chutneys. This recipe comes from the late great Jane Grigson's *Vegetable Book*, a volume I open every time I cook for company.

55g/2oz butter
3 tbsp grated mature Cheddar
2 tbsp Parmesan
6 beetroot, boiled, skinned and cubed
salt and freshly ground pepper
6 anchovy fillets
300ml/½ pint double cream
breadcrumbs

Butter a gratin dish and sprinkle a third of the cheese over it. Put in half the beetroot. Season well and spread over it another third of cheese, lay on the anchovy fillets, repeat with the rest of the beetroot and the cheese, packing in well. Pour over enough cream to come to the top of the beetroot. Scatter with a few breadcrumbs and dot with bits of butter. Bake for about 15 minutes in a fairly hot oven 200°C/400°F/Gas 6 until bubbling and golden brown.

CDW

Proper Bread Sauce

This much beloved sauce can be a terrible disappointment when served in hotels and restaurants and I'm afraid in many people's houses. The French have never seen the point of it, though I have made a few converts. It couldn't be simpler, the all important point being the flavouring of the milk. There is never enough sauce so make a lot. It is delicious served cold with the remains of a bird.

1 onion
10 cloves or more, to taste
600ml/1 pint full cream milk
25g/1oz butter
1 bayleaf
about 12–16 tbsp fresh white breadcrumbs, made from day-old good bread
300ml/½ pint double cream
salt and freshly ground pepper
freshly grated nutmeg

Peel the onion and stud it with the cloves. Place in a saucepan with the milk, butter and bayleaf. Bring to the boil and simmer on a low heat for 2 minutes. Remove from the heat, cover and let it steep all day to absorb the flavours. When nearly ready to serve, heat again, then add the breadcrumbs a few tablespoons at a time until you get the right consistency, remembering that they will swell. (I make the breadcrumbs in a food processor which is fast and easy.) Add the cream, season well with salt and pepper and finally with a good scraping of nutmeg. Remove the onion and bayleaf, transfer to a well warmed sauce-boat and serve with whatever you had in mind.

JP

Hoppin' John

This is a very comforting dish, probably from the Caribbean where they have a passion for blackeyed peas. Eat it on its own or as an accompaniment to any meat you might fancy.

225g/8oz blackeyed beans
225g/8oz salt bacon, cut into lardons
1 medium onion, finely chopped
2 cloves of garlic, crushed
4 tomatoes, skinned, deseeded and coarsely chopped
1 bayleaf
pinch of thyme
2 tsp cayenne pepper
salt and freshly ground black pepper
150g/6oz long grain rice

Soak the blackeyed beans overnight in cold water. Strain the beans, put in a saucepan and cover with cold water, add 1 teaspoon of salt, bring to the boil and boil rapidly for 10 minutes, then reduce the heat and simmer for about 1 hour. Fry the bacon and set aside. Fry the onion and garlic until soft, not brown, in the residual bacon fat then add the tomatoes, fry lightly for 1 minute. Add the onion, garlic, tomatoes, bacon, bayleaf, thyme, cayenne and black pepper to the cooked blackeyed beans and taste for salt. Cook for a further 20 minutes, the water should have evaporated by this time. In the meantime, cook the rice and add to the blackeyed bean mixture. Transfer to a serving dish.

JP

Broad Beans with Dill

I love broad beans, but sadly in Britain we tend to discard the pods which are sometimes better than the beans themselves. My father had many Egyptian contacts as he was involved in the setting up of the Anglo-American hospital in Cairo. He loved their food and regularly had pigeons and mullet roe sent from Cairo. His friend Dr Halim Grace gave him this recipe.

900g/2lb young fresh broad beans in their pods
150ml/¼ pint olive oil
2 onions, chopped
2 cloves of garlic, peeled and finely chopped
2 tbsp lemon juice
salt
½ tsp sugar
300ml/½ pint boiling water
2 tbsp freshly chopped dill
300ml/½ pint Greek yoghurt

Wash the beans, top, tail and string them where necessary. Heat the oil in a large, heavy, lidded pan. Sauté the onions and garlic to soften. Reduce heat, add the beans in their pods and the lemon juice and season with salt and sugar. Stir, and stew gently for 15 minutes stirring occasionally. Add water and half the dill, adjust to a gentle simmer and cook for 1 hour until the pods are very tender. Leave to cool. Pour the lot into a dish with the rest of the dill. Serve with the yoghurt and hot pitta bread. This dish improves with keeping.

CDW

Broad Bean Pod Purée

This is another delicious way of using the broad bean pods which you may normally throw away. The purée is very good with ham and you can enclose some in a slice to make an interesting canapé or cold buffet dish.

900g/2lb broad bean pods
water
salt and freshly ground pepper
1 tbsp butter

Top and tail your pods and simmer in a large pan of salted water until they are tender, about 20–30 minutes depending on their age. Drain and either put through the mouli or purée in a blender. Season and reheat with the butter.

CDW

Cauliflower with Almond Sauce

This is a Spanish recipe and makes an interesting change to the usual white sauce. The tip about the bayleaf is one of the most useful things the Cordon Bleu taught me, be careful not to throw it away until you have drained the cauliflower.

1 medium cauliflower
1 bayleaf
25g/1oz butter
55g/2oz flour
300ml/½ pint milk
salt
2 tbsp ground almonds
½ tsp chilli powder

Cook the cauliflower with the bayleaf to prevent odour. Melt the butter, stir in the flour and gradually add the milk, then the almonds, salt and chilli powder. Cook until the sauce thickens, stirring for 1 minute or more, if too thick add more milk. Put the cauliflower in a serving dish and pour over the sauce, sprinkle with toasted almond flakes and serve.

CDW

Sardinian Artichoke Pie

Globe artichokes are very Elizabethan. I know they don't grow too well over here, so snap them up when you see them. Out of season, they are good in jars and any delicatessen worth its salt should have them. This makes a good vegetarian main course as well as an excellent supper dish or starter.

28 artichoke hearts or 12 baby artichokes
150g/6oz white breadcrumbs
225g/8oz grated Parmesan cheese
225g/8oz grated Romano cheese
3 tbsp capers, drained and chopped
3 tbsp olive oil
225g/8oz black olives, stoned and halved
5 medium tomatoes, peeled and thinly sliced
or 1 large can plum tomatoes, drained and chopped
275g/10oz Fontina or Gruyère thinly sliced

If using whole baby artichokes, trim the leaves, boil until tender and slice thinly. Butter a 25cm/10in spring cake tin and coat with one third of the breadcrumbs. In a bowl mix the Parmesan, Romano and remaining breadcrumbs. Arrange layers in the cake tin beginning with the artichokes, following with capers and olives, tomatoes, Fontina and then the breadcrumb mixture. Drizzle 1 tablespoon olive oil over this and repeat, pressing down well. This should make three layers. Bake in a preheated oven 180°C/350°F/Gas 4 for 25 minutes. Leave to cool for 10 minutes, unmould and serve with salad.

CDW

Broccoli with Corn and Chorizo Sauce

Like the former American President George Bush I am not that fond of broccoli, although I love purple sprouting broccoli. However it is sometimes the only green vegetable around and this is a good way of enlivening it. If you want to make it more substantial, you can add more chorizo sausage and have it as a supper dish.

750g /1½lb broccoli
115g/4 oz butter
4 shallots, chopped
450g/1lb corn kernels
2 tbsp water
pinch of nutmeg
115g/4oz chorizo sausage, chopped
salt and freshly ground pepper

Separate the broccoli into florets. Melt 55g/2oz butter in a pan, add the broccoli and stir to coat with butter. Add water to cover and cook for about 10 minutes or until just tender, but still crunchy. In a pan melt the remaining butter, add shallots and corn and cook until the shallots are soft. In a food processor blend this mixture adding a little water. Return to the pan, add the nutmeg, sausage and seasonings, and gently heat through. Thin if too thick and pour over the broccoli.

CDW

Tomato Tart

A tomato tart looks wonderful with its dramatic colours. This is really a left-over salad Niçoise that I put into a pie crust one day. If you use a piece of fresh tuna it is even better and more sophisticated.

FOR THE SHORTCRUST PASTRY:
115g/4oz plain flour
25g/1oz butter
25g/1oz lard
1 tbsp freshly grated Parmesan cheese (optional)
salt
cold water

FOR THE FILLING:
450g/1lb tomatoes
2 tbsp olive oil
1 clove of garlic, finely chopped
1 medium onion, finely chopped
1 tsp oregano
salt and freshly ground pepper
6 anchovy fillets, chopped or small can of tuna or 115g/4oz piece of fresh tuna
25g/1oz strong Cheddar, grated
2 large eggs
150ml/¼ pint single cream
25g/1oz stoned black olives, chopped

Sift the flour and salt together and rub in the butter and lard until the mixture resembles breadcrumbs. Add the cheese and bind with a little cold water. Chill for 30 minutes and then roll out to line a 20cm/8in flan dish. Chill again for 30 minutes. Cover with foil and baking beans and bake blind in a preheated oven at 200°C/400°F/Gas 6 for 10 minutes. Remove foil and baking beans and cook for a further 5 minutes.

Peel the tomatoes, deseed, slice, strain and save the juice. In a small pan heat the oil over a low heat and sauté the onion until soft, add the garlic and oregano and cook for 1 minute. Add the tomato juice, season and cook till the juice is almost absorbed. Put this in the pastry case and cover with fish. If you are using fresh tuna cook it in a pan with a little more oil for about 2 minutes turning as necessary, then flake it. Cover with tomatoes and grated cheese. Whisk the eggs with the cream and pour over the tomatoes, scattering the olives on top. Bake in a preheated oven at 200°C/400°F/Gas 6 for 15–20 minutes. Serve hot or cold with a green salad, or a salad of green beans, or deep fried French beans which you have dipped in batter.

CDW

Illustrated overleaf

French Beans with Bacon and Tomato

A variation on the ever-popular French bean. This can be used as a side dish or even as a first course, or as an addition to pasta.

150g/6oz diced bacon
300ml/½ pint stock
750g/1½lb French beans
5 medium tomatoes, peeled, de-seeded and coarsely chopped
salt and fresh ground black pepper
1 tbsp chopped parsley

Put the bacon and stock into a pan, bring to the boil and simmer bacon for 20 minutes, then add the beans, tomatoes and black pepper. Taste for salt as it should not be necessary to add any unless the bacon is very mild. Bring back to the boil and simmer over a low heat until the beans are cooked. Strain the beans, bacon and tomatoes into a serving dish. The beans may lose a bit of colour but their flavour will be enhanced. Sprinkle with parsley and serve.

JP

Swiss Chard with Garlic and Anchovies

I adore Swiss chard and it grew very profusely on the pheasant farm where I cooked. This is a good way of using the stalks.

900g/2 lb Swiss chard, with white stalks
2 tbsp olive oil
4 cloves of garlic
1 small can anchovies
freshly ground black pepper

Wash the chard. Cut off the white stalks and trim their ends and any discoloured portions. Heat the oil in a covered pan and add the garlic and anchovies, allow this to cook until the anchovies have melted into the oil, about 5 minutes. Cut the chard stalks into 2.5cm/1in pieces, blanch them in boiling water and refresh under a cold tap. Drain well, add them to the oil and season with the pepper. Cover and cook gently for 10 minutes. If you wish you may add the chard greens at this stage and cook for a further 3–5 minutes or you may wish to use the greens for something else.

CDW

Couscous Salad

Couscous seems to be appearing everywhere these days, so voilà.

150g/6oz couscous
1 red pepper, skinned, deseeded and chopped
1 yellow pepper, skinned, deseeded and chopped
4 spring onions, finely chopped
3 tomatoes, skinned, deseeded and chopped
1 tbsp chopped parsley
1 tbsp chopped olives

FOR THE DRESSING:
4 tbsp virgin olive oil
grated zest and juice of ½ a lemon
1 clove of garlic, crushed
salt and freshly ground pepper

Cook the couscous according to the packet instructions. When the grains have swollen, fold in the salad ingredients. Put the dressing ingredients in a lidded jar and shake vigorously. Pour over the couscous and mix well before turning into a serving dish.

JP

Hot Curried Cabbage

During the winter when there is a poor variety of fresh vegetables and a lot of cabbage, this makes an interesting way of dealing with that estimable, if somewhat dull, vegetable.

½ a large cabbage, shredded
1 bayleaf
2 cloves of garlic
250ml/8fl oz stock
1 onion
2 cloves
flour
salt and freshly ground pepper
1 tbsp curry powder
3 tbsp butter
120ml/4fl oz cream
55g/2oz dried breadcrumbs

Put the cabbage in a large pan, add the stock, bayleaf and garlic. Stick the cloves into the onion and add to the cabbage. Cook over a medium heat for 10 minutes. Drain the cabbage and discard the bayleaf and the onion. Put the cabbage into a greased casserole dish. Mix together salt, pepper, curry powder and half the butter, add cream and stir until smooth. Pour over the cabbage. Sprinkle on breadcrumbs, dot with remaining butter and bake at 180°C/350°F/Gas 4 for 20 minutes.

CDW

Jerusalem Artichokes with Fine Herbs

This is a delicious vegetable dish, particularly good with poultry or even game. I love it, although its disadvantage is that it tends to create quite a lot of wind, but never mind.

450g/1lb artichokes, peeled and rinsed
salt and freshly ground pepper
2 shallots, finely chopped
1 clove of garlic, finely chopped
25g/1oz butter
1 tbsp flour
300ml/½ pint milk
pinch of grated nutmeg
½ tbsp chopped chives
1 tbsp chopped parsley

Cut the artichokes into evenly sized pieces, cover with water in a saucepan, add a teaspoon of salt, bring to the boil and simmer for about 30 minutes. Check to see if they are cooked, then strain. Meanwhile melt the butter in a saucepan, cook the shallots and garlic gently until they are soft but not coloured. Blend in the flour with a wooden spoon, add the milk gradually, stirring constantly, then add the grated nutmeg. When the sauce has thickened to a nice consistency add a ¼ teaspoon of pepper, chives and most of the parsley, and stir into the artichokes. Sprinkle remaining parsley over the whole mixture.

JP

Mushrooms with Chicken Livers

When I was young chicken livers were an enormous treat and I still think of them as such. Luckily they are freely available nowadays. It is terribly important to keep the little livers pink on the inside, otherwise they will become tough and crumbly. Always make sure the bile duct is removed.

450g/1lb mushrooms, sliced
225g/8oz chicken livers
1 medium onion, thinly sliced
1 clove of garlic, crushed
25g/1oz butter
1 tbsp olive oil
salt and freshly ground pepper
300ml/½ pint dry white wine
4 tbsp balsamic vinegar
1 tbsp chopped parsley

Fry the onion and garlic in the butter and oil until they are lightly coloured. Add the mushrooms and fry until they are softened. Chop the chicken livers into bite-size pieces and add to the mushrooms. Cook for about 3–4 minutes and season with salt and pepper. Put the wine and balsamic vinegar in a saucepan and reduce by half, add the chopped parsley and pour over the chicken livers. Serve with hot toast.

JP

Stuffed Onion Rolls

This is a Saudi Arabian dish and was adapted from that curious book *Memory Recipes of Desert Storm* which was published following the Gulf War. I met the author, Monica Gabur, and it is the only time I have ever tried to negotiate with someone in full purdah. Not easy I can tell you. The recipe is a bit fiddly but worth the effort, unlike another recipe 'Lamp feet with toes' which turned out to be lamb's trotters with toast!

4 large onions
450g/1lb minced lamb
1 tbsp chopped parsley
1 tsp cinnamon
½ tsp allspice
200g/7oz chopped tomatoes
3 tbsp dried breadcrumbs
salt and freshly ground pepper
1 tsp sugar
juice of ½ a lemon
1 tbsp oil

Peel the onions carefully, cutting off the root ends. Cut one half of the onion from top to bottom leaving the other half intact. Put in a saucepan of boiling water and simmer for 10 minutes. Drain cool and separate carefully into layers. Mix together the cinnamon, allspice, mince, tomatoes and breadcrumbs and add seasoning. Place a tablespoon of the stuffing on each onion slice and roll up tightly. Line the bottom of a heavy saucepan with the unused onion pieces. Pack in the rolls closely, seam side down. Mix sugar and lemon juice with half a cup of water and pour over the rolls. Top with the oil. Place a small upturned saucer or plate over the rolls to prevent unrolling. Simmer gently over a low heat for 1 hour adding water if necessary. Transfer to a serving plate.

CDW

Peas with Lettuce

Test the peas occasionally for taste and tenderness. I often add chopped spring onions to this receipt, but this is optional.

85g/3oz of butter
1.2litre/2pints fresh shelled peas
2 lettuce hearts, tied up with string
1 bouquet garni
1½ tsp salt
2 tsp sugar
3 tbsp water
150ml/¼ pint double cream

Melt the butter in a saucepan, add peas, lettuce hearts, bouquet garni, salt, sugar and water. Simmer with the lid on for 40 minutes. Remove lettuce and strain peas, reserving the liquid. The amount of liquid should be very little but reduce it to about two tablespoonfuls, whisk in the cream and pour over peas. Cut lettuce hearts into quarters and place on the peas.

JP

Salad of Lettuce Hearts

Make sure that your hearts are nice and firm and you won't go wrong with this simple salad.

Some good lettuce hearts
bunch of watercress
½ punnet of cress
1 hard-boiled egg

FOR THE FRENCH DRESSING:
4 tbsp virgin olive oil
1 tbsp wine vinegar
salt and freshly ground pepper

Arrange the lettuce hearts in a salad bowl and sprinkle over with finely chopped watercress leaves and cut cress. Separate the white of the egg from the yolk, and sieve both. Then sprinkle over the salad. Put the ingredients of the French dressing in a lidded jar and shake vigorously. Pour over the salad before serving.

JP

Spinach and Rice

A great comfort, and so good for you too.

2 tbsp virgin olive oil
4 shallots, finely chopped
1 large clove of garlic
150g/6oz long grain rice,
cooked
150g/6oz spinach, cooked,
drained and liquidised
1 tbsp mint, finely chopped
½ tsp cinnamon
salt and freshly ground pepper

Heat the olive oil in a frying pan, add the shallots and garlic and cook for a few minutes to soften, don't brown or burn. Add rice to frying pan, stir and coat with the oil. Add spinach, mint, cinnamon, salt and pepper and stir. Cook until the contents of the pan are heated through.

JP

Pete's Pommy Pommes

This comes from a magnificent Australian friend, Pete Smith, and my nickname for them is Pommy Pommes. Pete served them at a dinner party with roast lamb, but I have used them with game where they are perfect and easier than proper game chips. Not enough is made of potatoes and I think everyone would love this crunchy, succulent method.

450g/1lb waxy potatoes, peeled
olive oil
150ml/¼ pint vegetable or chicken stock
salt and freshly ground pepper
herbs of your choice (parsley, thyme, tarragon, etc.)
4 cloves of garlic, finely chopped

Slice the potatoes very finely on a mandolin, or with a good, sharp knife or a processor. Steep in cold water for 30 minutes, drain and pat dry. There should only be about 5 layers of potatoes, so choose your roasting pan accordingly. Drizzle some olive oil over the base of the pan. Put a layer of overlapping potato slices on the base, season with salt and freshly ground pepper, a sprinkling of herbs and garlic, a drizzle of olive oil and moisten with a little stock. Continue in this manner until everything is used up. Place in a pre-heated oven at 190°C/375°F/Gas 5 until softish when pierced, then increase the heat to 230°C/450°F/Gas 8 until very brown and crisp. Serve with what you will.

JP

Potato Dumplings with Chanterelles

Chanterelles grow freely in Scotland, indeed there were so many last year that my friends Charles and Anne Fraser sent me a box by post from their Highland retreat. Some people make the mistake of using too-strong flavours with these delicate mushrooms but this dish suits them very well. It is an excellent accompaniment to roast meat or stews and a good supper dish on its own.

750g/1½lb potatoes, peeled
115g/4oz plain flour
1 egg
1 egg yolk
salt and freshly ground pepper
140g/5oz cottage cheese
140g/5oz chanterelles or other wild mushrooms
55g/2oz butter
3 shallots, minced
extra softened butter for brushing

Boil and mash the potatoes and mix in the flour, egg and the yolk and salt to taste and allow the heat to cook them. Sieve the cheese and drain it. Clean and chop the mushrooms, and sauté them in the butter with the shallots. Allow the mushrooms and shallots to cool slightly and mix in the cheese.

Roll the potato into a sausage and cut into 16 parts, roll these into balls. Make an indentation in each ball and stuff with the mushroom mixture pinching the potato round the filling to seal it. Bring a large pan of salt water to the boil and poach the dumplings for 10 minutes, drain them well and allow to cool. Heat the grill, brush each dumpling with a little melted butter and grill till brown.

CDW

Sugar Browned Potatoes

This is a different way of serving new potatoes and is particularly good with the tasteless new potatoes you buy out of season or you know where! Do not, for instance, waste Jersey royals on this recipe. It is also a good way for re-heating cooked left over new potatoes.

900g/2lb new potatoes
55g/2oz butter
2 tbsp sugar

Scrape the potatoes and cook until tender. Do not under or over-cook, either is a crime.

In a heavy pan melt the butter, add the sugar and cook over a low heat until the sugar begins to caramelise. Add the potatoes and make sure they become well coated in the caramel. Continue this process until the caramel is a good rich brown. Serve at once.

CDW

PUDDINGS (AND CAKES)

Picnicking in Cambridge

Many a bad meal has been saved by a good pudding. It is the last thing one goes away remembering and sometimes, when a meal is consistently bad, you find yourself waiting for the bought ice-cream you know will inevitably follow. I think of the puddings we have served on the programme over the series and how well they have been received. It is good to make a pudding specially to fit like, Jennifer's Peaches Cardinal Hume for the priests at Westminster Cathedral, but one must avoid the danger of falling into the trap of becoming like an Edwardian chef and naming every pudding for one's friends.

Another approach to puddings is an adaptation of the familiar to surprise, like my Christmas Pudding Ice-cream Bombe, which I made for the Winchester choirboys on our first Christmas special. To digress slightly, due to the constraints of

time I was not allowed the easier intermittent step of freezing the two halves of the bombe before inserting the brandy butter centre and closing the bombe. 'Slap it together,' said Pat Llewellyn, our wild Welsh director. With an over-heated Aga behind me and the arc lamps heating the air in front, my bombe was melting rapidly and I was acutely conscious that had my aim missed, the bishop would have had to redecorate his kitchen.

My friend Angus Hamilton is so fond of ice-cream that he loaned me the vintage ice cream maker I used at Winchester so that in return I might design him an ice-cream; testing is still in progress. One friend, a recovering alcoholic like me, desperately missed eating trifle, so I had the interesting chore of designing a sherry-free trifle which I finally achieved with a mixture of orange juice and balsamic vinegar!

Almond and Semolina Custard

Even at school, where I was scorned for it, I liked semolina and, as an adult, I like this pudding for its subtle sophisticated flavour. I have weaned many people from their childhood aversion with this dish, so do try it please.

2 tbsp butter
150g/6oz almonds, blanched and flaked
150g/6oz fine semolina
115g/4oz sugar
900ml/1½ pints milk
1 tsp lemon zest
cinnamon

Heat butter gently in a saucepan. Toss in almonds and fry until they begin to colour, add semolina and stir over the heat until it begins to colour. In another pan dissolve the sugar in the milk, bring to the boil and add lemon zest. Pour milk over the semolina and almonds, allow to thicken stirring constantly, and cook for a further minute. Pour the mixture on to saucers, sprinkle with cinnamon and serve warm.

CDW

Peasant Girl with Veil

Not a dish for the average peasant girl, I wouldn't think, except maybe in Normandy. There she could find her apples and her Calvados which can be used instead of brandy, and good luck to her.

2 heaped tbsp brown
breadcrumbs
55g/2oz butter
750g/1½lb apples, peeled,
cored and sliced
2 scant tbsp brown sugar
1 tbsp brandy
300ml/½ pint double cream,
whipped
115g/4oz dark chocolate,
grated

Fry breadcrumbs in butter until golden brown. Cook the apples with the brown sugar in a little water and when cooked stir in the brandy. In a glass dish arrange alternate layers of breadcrumbs and apples, finishing with a layer of breadcrumbs. Cover the top layer with the whipped double cream and sprinkle the grated chocolate over the top.

JP

Apple Balls

This is a Dutch recipe given to me by my Dutch godmother. You should not use cooking apples as they are purely a Victorian English invention and are designed to collapse. For this dish you need fruit that will keep its shape.

550g/1¼lb plain flour
pinch of salt
150g/6oz unsalted butter
2 eggs
120ml/4fl oz sour cream
6 apples
2 tbsp sugar
2 tsp cinnamon
55g/2oz sultanas
2 tbsp butter

Sift flour and salt into a bowl and rub in the butter to the bread-crumb stage. Beat together 1 egg and the cream and add to the flour. Mix to form a dough and knead, then wrap in plastic and chill for 30 minutes.

Peel and core the apples, mix together the sugar, cinnamon and sultanas. Stuff each apple with a little of the sugar mixture and add a small piece of butter.

Roll out the pastry, cut into six squares each large enough to enclose an apple. Wrap each apple in its pastry overcoat and bind the join with beaten egg. Place on a greased baking tray and bake at 190°C/370°F/Gas 5 until golden brown, about 30 minutes.

CDW

Apple Strudel

You will find this famous national dish in every cake shop and cafe in Austria and Germany, not to mention Soho. Don't be frightened by the filo pastry, it is quite easy to manage as long as you keep it moist. I prefer to use Bramley apples for strudel.

450g/1lb of cooking apples, peeled, cored and cut into thin slices
55g/2oz caster sugar
½ tsp cinnamon
40g/1½oz sultanas
40g/1½oz walnuts, finely chopped
1 tsp grated lemon rind
8 sheets filo pastry
85g/3oz melted butter
2 tbsp white breadcrumbs

In a mixing bowl, combine apples, caster sugar, cinnamon, sultanas, walnuts and lemon rind. Keep the filo pastry covered with a damp cloth to prevent it drying out. Lay a sheet of filo pastry on a damp cloth, brush with melted butter and cover with a thin layer of breadcrumbs. Put another sheet of filo pastry on top and repeat the process. Arrange a 2.5cm/1in thick roll of apple mixture 5cm/2in from the end of the filo pastry nearest to you. Lift up the end of the damp cloth nearest you, the filo pastry will begin to roll over. Firm the filo over the apple mixture and then continue to roll to get a jam roll effect. Repeat with the rest of the filo and apple mixture. Bake in a preheated oven at 220°C/425°F/Gas 7 for 10 minutes, then reduce the heat to 200°C/400°F/Gas 6 and cook for a further 20 minutes, or until the strudel is crisp and brown.

JP

Quercyan Apple Cake

Usually I keep my recipes very simple but this, though somewhat harder than usual, really repays the effort. Most of my stay in Quercy is either unremembered or censored, but the recipe remains.

450g/1lb plain flour
½ tsp baking powder
2 eggs
40g/1½oz butter, creamed

FOR THE FILLING:
1.5kg/3lb apples, peeled and
thinly sliced
225g/8oz sugar
120ml/4fl oz rum
85ml/3fl oz orange flower
water
thinly pared rind of 1 lemon

TO FINISH:
25g/1oz butter, melted
1 egg, beaten
caster sugar

Macerate the sliced apples with the filling ingredients overnight. Strain the apples, reserving the juice.

Sift the flour and baking powder into a large bowl, put butter and eggs into a well in the centre. Working with the fingertips gradually add 200ml/7fl oz of the liquid from the apples. Work into a smooth and elastic paste with your hand and leave to rest for 2 hours. Roll out as thinly as possible, then transfer to a floured cloth on a large table. Working from the centre, with the palms of your hands, carefully stretch the paste to the thinness of a cigarette paper. Rest it and yourself for 1 hour.

Brush lightly with melted butter and dust with sugar, cover with well drained apples and roll up. Mix the remaining juice into the beaten egg and brush over the top. Bake in a preheated oven at 190°C/390°F/Gas 5 for 50–55 minutes.

CDW

Apricot Mousse

You will certainly feel like the tipsy pussycat who has got the cream after consuming this delectable mousse.

225g/½lb dried or no soak apricots
55g/2oz sugar
25g/1oz blanched, slivered almonds
few drops of vanilla essence
120ml/4fl oz double cream
1 tbsp Cointreau, Curaçao or any other flavoured liqueur, or brandy
Langue de Chat biscuits

Barely cover apricots with water, add sugar, bring to the boil, lower heat and simmer for about 30 minutes. If 'no soak' apricots are used, just cover with boiling water, add sugar and stir until sugar has dissolved. Purée apricots with the liquid, add the liqueur and the vanilla essence, fold in the whipped cream and slivered almonds. Spoon into individual glasses and chill. Before serving sprinkle with a few more slivered almonds, another blob of cream and Langue de Chat biscuits.

JP

Cheese and Honey Pie

The Greeks love honey sweet desserts. This one may not be to everybody's taste but goes well with the addition of a tart fruit salad on the side.

115g/4oz shortcrust pastry
225g/8oz low fat cheese, such as ricotta
3 tbsp honey
2 eggs, well beaten
juice of ½ a lemon
1 tsp cinnamon
115g/4oz walnuts, crushed

Preheat oven to 180°C/350°F/Gas 4. Line a 20cm/8in flan dish with the pastry and bake blind for 10 minutes. While flan is cooking, mix the cheese with the honey. Add eggs, lemon juice and half the cinnamon and mix thoroughly. Cover the flan base with walnuts and pour the mixture on top. Cook for 30 minutes in a preheated moderate oven at 190°C/375°F/Gas 5. Make sure the mixture is set and then sprinkle the remaining cinnamon on top.

JP

Hot Chocolate Soufflé

Nobody can resist chocolate soufflé unless they're allergic. If you wish you can make just one large soufflé in which case it would take about 30 minutes to cook.

85g/3oz good quality dark chocolate
1 tbsp brandy or rum
25g/1oz butter
25g/1oz plain flour
150ml/¼ pint milk
70g/2½ oz caster sugar
½ tsp vanilla extract
4 eggs, separated

Break up the chocolate and put in a bowl with the brandy or rum. Put the bowl over a saucepan of gently simmering water and allow to melt slowly.

Melt the butter in a saucepan, add the flour and cook over a low heat for a few minutes, stirring constantly. Warm the milk in another saucepan, melt the caster sugar in it and then blend in to the flour and butter. Continue to cook slowly, stirring constantly, until the mixture thickens. Remove the saucepan from the heat, add the vanilla extract and chocolate mixture and mix well. Add the lightly beaten egg yolks and beat well. Whisk the egg whites fairly stiffly and then fold into the chocolate mixture.

Spoon the mixture into individual buttered ramekin dishes and bake in a preheated oven 190°C/375°F/Gas 5 for about 15 minutes or until the soufflés are well risen. Serve immediately.

JP

Chocolate Crème Brulée

Everybody loves crème brulée, and some people are seriously addicted to chocolate. I dedicate this recipe to Rebekka Hardy, who not only made me a better cook, but also made me think about chocolate 24 hours a day.

600ml/1 pint double cream
1 vanilla pod, split
300g/11oz plain dark chocolate
4 medium egg yolks
55g/2oz icing sugar, sifted
3 tbsp caster sugar

In a heavy pan heat the cream with the vanilla pod until scalding hot but not boiling. Remove from heat, cover and leave to infuse for 15 minutes. Remove the pod and scrape seeds into the cream with the tip of a knife. Break up the chocolate and stir into the cream until melted and smooth.

Put the egg yolks and icing sugar into a bowl. Beat with a wooden spoon until well blended and then stir in chocolate cream. Pour into ramekin dishes. Stand in a bain-marie. Bake in a preheated oven at 180°C/350°F/Gas 4 for 30 minutes until firm. Remove and cool. Chill overnight or for up to 48 hours. Sprinkle caster sugar over the top and put under a hot grill to caramelise. Serve within 1 hour.

CDW

Chocolate Egg Snowball

This is a variation on what I call *Oafs à la Neigh*. I once had a dearly loved employer who was addicted to chocolate. 'It's just like your gin, dear,' she would say as she sent me to the village shop at midnight. I spent a lot of time adapting recipes to include chocolate!

115g/4oz plain chocolate
6 eggs, separated
30ml/2 tbsp caster sugar
900ml/1½ pints full cream milk
115g/4oz sugar

Melt the chocolate over hot water. Beat the egg whites until very stiff. Add the 30ml/2 tbsp caster sugar and whisk again until stiff and the sugar is dissolved. Bring the milk to a simmering point in a wide flat pan. Shape the egg white mass into a round flat cake and poach this gently in the simmering milk for a few minutes, turn it carefully with a fish slice and poach the other side. Leave to drain on kitchen paper or a clean cloth.

Beat the egg yolks and half the sugar into the melted chocolate and pour the slightly cooled milk over the mixture. Place over hot (not boiling) water in a double boiler. Cook stirring constantly until the mixture thickens to the consistency of thin cream. Pour into a glass bowl and place the egg whites on top. Chill.

Ten minutes before serving, caramelise the remaining sugar in a thick saucepan and pour over the egg whites.

CDW

Coconut Blancmange with Cranberry Sauce

A pale and interesting pudding with a dramatic red sauce. Even those who dread the word blancmange will like the coconut effect, I hope. My various sojourns in the West Indies have left me with a taste for the fruit and a large supply of recipes.

350g/12oz desiccated coconut
1.2 litres/2 pints milk
6 tbsp cornflour
115g/4oz caster sugar
115g/4oz cranberries
55g/2oz sugar
juice of ½ a lemon

Put the coconut and milk in a saucepan and heat to a simmering point. Remove from the heat and stand for 30 minutes for the flavour to infuse. Strain through a cheesecloth, pressing to extract all the liquid.

Put the cornflour in a large bowl and blend to a smooth paste with some of the coconut milk. Put the rest of the coconut milk and caster sugar in a pan, heat gently until the sugar dissolves then bring to the boil. Pour quickly over the cornflour, stirring briskly. Return to the heat and stir until large bubbles break the surface. Pour into a wetted mould, cool to room temperature, chill and unmould. Heat the cranberries with the sugar and lemon juice and pour over the blancmange.

CDW

Zuppa Inglese

This curious Italian name, making you think of soup, is in fact a good old fashioned English trifle, far removed from the sort of thing you used to get in the nursery. The Italians took it to their hearts and have loved it ever since.

4 egg yolks
4 tbsp sugar
1 tsp vanilla essence
40g/1½oz plain flour, sifted
tiny pinch of salt
600ml/1 pint milk
150ml/¼ pint Marsala
1 sponge cake, sliced crosswise into three layers
85g/3oz chocolate, grated

Put egg yolks in a bowl, gradually add sugar and vanilla essence, cream well, add flour, pinch of salt and 150ml/¼ pint milk. Boil remaining milk, pour on to the mixture in the bowl, stir well and return to the saucepan. Simmer gently, stirring constantly for about 3–4 minutes. Pour a third of the mixture into a bowl, add 55g/2oz of grated chocolate and stir until chocolate has melted. Leave both mixtures to cool.

Place a layer of sponge cake on a serving dish, sprinkle with Marsala and cover with a layer of plain custard. Add another layer of sponge, more Marsala and cover with the chocolate custard. Add the last layer of sponge, sprinkle with Marsala and cover with the remaining plain custard. Sprinkle the remaining chocolate over the custard.

JP

Omelette Stephanie

Everyone knows of the Austrian Crown Prince Rudolph and his suicide pact with his mistress Maria Vetsera at Mayerling. There have been plays, novels and even a ballet on the theme. Prince Rudolph had a wife, the Crown Princess Stephanie, whose legacy is this delicious soufflé omelette.

2 tbsp butter
4 egg whites, stiffly beaten
3 egg yolks
3 tbsp icing sugar
3 tbsp double cream
2 level tbsp plain flour
1 punnet of raspberries

Melt the butter in a fireproof dish, and turn it to spread the butter evenly. Beat the egg yolks with 2 tablespoons of icing sugar until the mixture is pale and forms ribbons. Beat in the double cream and the flour and fold this mixture into the egg whites. Slide carefully into the hot buttered dish. Cook in a preheated oven at 190°C/375°F/Gas 5 for just over 15 minutes.

Roll your raspberries in the remaining icing sugar. Slide the omelette onto a warm plate, put the raspberries on one side and fold over the omelette. Sprinkle with icing sugar and serve at once.

CDW

Plum Kuchen

This German delight is full of cream and plums and is very good with a cup of excellent coffee.

115g/4oz brown flour
pinch of baking powder
85g/3oz butter, softened
25g/1oz ground almonds
85g/3oz brown sugar
1 tbsp cinnamon
750g/1½lb ripe Victoria plums,
cut in half and stoned
2 egg yolks
150ml/¼ pint sour cream

Sift the flour and baking powder into a bowl, rub in the softened butter, add the almonds and 55g/2oz of the brown sugar, mix. Press the mixture firmly into a buttered 20–23cm/8-9in flan tin. Arrange the plums, flesh side down, to cover the mixture closely. Sprinkle with cinnamon and the remaining sugar. Bake in a pre-heated oven at 190°C/375°F/Gas 5 for 20–25 minutes.

In the meantime beat the egg yolks with the sour cream and when the plums have been brought out of the oven pour this mixture over the plums and then bake for a further 40 minutes, at the same temperature.

JP

Rich Vanilla Ice-Cream with Chocolate Puffs

My Belgian great aunt whose measurement round her waist when she married equalled the measurement round her neck when she died at the age of ninety-two prided herself on her vanilla ice-cream. I think you will enjoy it too.

FOR THE ICE-CREAM:
350ml/12fl oz full cream milk
1 vanilla pod, cut in half lengthways
85g/3oz caster sugar
5 egg yolks
175ml/6fl oz whipping cream (35% fat)

FOR THE CHOCOLATE PUFFS:
115g/4oz chocolate
8 egg whites
450g/1lb caster sugar

In a medium saucepan mix the milk, half the sugar and the vanilla pod to just below boiling point and set aside for at least 15 minutes to infuse. In a heat-proof bowl mix the egg yolks and the rest of the sugar, beating, preferably with an electric beater, until they reach the ribbon stage. Still beating pour on the scalded milk.

Now either place the bowl over boiling water or transfer the whole lot to a double boiler. Stirring frequently allow this to form a custard that coats the back of a spoon and holds a clear line. Remove from the heat and plunge immediately into cold water to arrest the cooking process. Transfer to a jug, cover and refrigerate till quite cool. Add the cream and mix well. Remove the vanilla pod, scrape out the seeds and add to the mixture, discarding the pod.

At this stage if you have an ice-cream maker churn the mixture for 15 minutes, if not transfer to the freezer stirring every 10 minutes until it is set. Serve with Scottish raspberries or other fresh fruit.

This chocolate biscuit recipe is, I think, the first and comes from my Patrick Lamb, which I bought myself at Sotheby's to celebrate my tenth sober birthday.

Melt the chocolate over hot water until soft and mix with the sugar. Mix the egg whites with a fork (do not whip them) and add to the chocolate and sugar to form a paste. Roll into pieces the size of walnuts. Place in tiny cake papers on a baking sheet covered with oiled greaseproof paper and cook in a slow oven at 140°C/275°F/ Gas 1 until crisp.

CDW

Christmas Pudding Ice-cream Bombe

This is the pudding I made for the Winchester choirboys in our first Christmas special. It is a lot easier to make if you are allowed to freeze each half when you have put the ice-cream in but before you put in the brandy butter centre, but then you won't have a perfectionist Welsh television director in your kitchen.

350ml/12fl oz milk
100g/3½oz soft brown sugar
3 egg yolks
175ml/6fl oz whipping cream, chilled
1 tbsp brandy
150g/6oz Christmas pudding, chopped
2 tbsp brandy butter
1 tbsp brandy, to serve

Put the milk and half the sugar in a medium saucepan and bring to just below boiling point. Put the egg yolks and remaining sugar in a bowl and beat until pale and forming ribbons. Bring milk back to the boil and pour in a thin stream on to egg yolks and sugar, whisking steadily. Pour into a double boiler and stir the custard until it thickens to from a clear line when coating the back of a spoon. Plunge the base of the pan into cold water. Transfer the custard to a jug, cover and chill. When the custard is cold, pour in the chilled cream.

Stir the brandy into the custard and churn in the ice-cream maker until it is the consistency of whipped cream, or transfer to the freezer, stirring every 10 minutes. Crumble in the pudding and churn for a further 5 seconds. Scrape into a box and freeze for 1-2 hours. Fill the chilled bombe moulds and freeze. Top with the brandy butter and close the bombe. Allow to freeze hard. Turn out, pour over the brandy and ignite.

CDW

Rhum Babas

This is an outrageously sticky pudding, soaking in rum and covered in syrup – a good heart stopper.
It was one of my mother's favourite delicacies and she lived to eighty-eight.

25g/1oz fresh yeast
150ml/¼ pint warm milk
225g/8oz strong flour
pinch of salt
55g/2oz caster sugar
3 eggs, beaten
55g/2oz butter, softened
85g/3oz sultanas
pinch of salt
300ml/½ pint freshly whipped cream, to serve

FOR THE SYRUP:
300ml/½ pint water
225g/8oz sugar
6 tbsp rum

Blend yeast, milk and 55g/2oz of the flour in a bowl and leave to stand in a warm place until frothy. Sift the remaining flour and salt into a large bowl and add the caster sugar. Make a well in the centre and add the frothy yeast mixture and mix with a wooden spoon. Gradually beat in the eggs and softened butter. Beat the mixture well, then cover with a cloth and leave to rise until double in bulk. Punch down the dough and knead in the sultanas. Put the dough into small greased ring moulds, half filling them, and leave to rise again until the dough is level with the top of the mould. Cook in a preheated oven at 200°C/400°F/Gas 6 for 15–20 minutes.

To make the syrup, dissolve the sugar in the water over a gentle heat for a few minutes, then stir in the rum. When the babas are cooked, leave them to cool in the moulds for a few minutes, then turn out and immerse in hot syrup. Remove from the syrup and serve with freshly-whipped cream.

JP

A Tart of Strawberries

Until the discovery of the new world all we had were the little *fraise de bois* or wild strawberries. It took the French to take the red Virginia strawberry, cross it with the large yellow Peruvian and breed on a different continent what we think of as strawberries. This is a seventeenth century recipe from Kenelm Digby, but none the worse for surviving the centuries.

FOR THE PASTRY:
225g/8oz flour
pinch of salt
115g/4oz butter
115g/4oz lard
zest of 1 orange
a little water

FOR THE FILLING:
115g/4oz caster sugar
½ tsp cinnamon
1 tsp ginger
2 punnets strawberries

To make the pastry, sift the flour and salt together and rub in the butter and lard until the mixture resembles fine crumbs. You can use all butter to make the pastry, but the combination of butter and lard makes a crisper crust. Stir in the orange zest and only a little water. This is very short so chill it well before rolling out. Use a pastry cutter to cut out linings and lids for individual tart tins.

Mix together the caster sugar, cinnamon and ginger, put your strawberries into the cases and sprinkle with this mixture. Cover with a lid, sprinkle on a little more sugar mixture and bake in a preheated oven at 190°C/375°F/Gas 5 for 15 minutes.

CDW

Fragomammella (Strawberry Breasts)

(formula by the Futurist Poet of National Record Farfa)

A pink plate with two erect feminine breasts made of ricotta dyed pink with Campari with nipples of candied strawberry. More fresh strawberries under the covering of ricotta, making it possible to bite into an ideal multiplication of imaginary breasts.

From *Futurist Cookbook* by Filippo Tommaso Marinetti
Published by Trefoil Publications Ltd, 7 Royal Parade, London SW6
© Estate of F.T. Marinetti, 1989
English translation ©Suzanne Brill, 1989

450g/1lb strawberries
1 tbsp lemon juice
1 tbsp caster sugar
550g/1¼lb ricotta cheese, fresh
150ml/¼ pint double cream
3 tbsp Campari
4–5 tbsp icing sugar

Set aside 16 of the smallest strawberries and cut the rest into small pieces. Put in a bowl with the lemon juice and caster sugar and leave to soak for 1 hour. Push the ricotta through the smallest sieve of a mouli, add cream and Campari, mix well. Sieve the icing sugar into the mixture to your own taste, put a third of the mixture aside and mix the strawberries into the remaining ricotta.

Prepare pink dessert plates and divide the mixture into 16 breast-shaped moulds, 2 for each plate. With a moistened spatula smooth the reserved ricotta over the moulds and place a strawberry on the top of each 'breast'. You can make the moulds 3 hours in advance and store in a refrigerator.

JP

Raspberry Shortcake

This is not shortcake in the Scottish sense but more the American variety which is really like a sponge cake that soaks up all the juices from the berries. Good and gooey, a delight to all children and grown-ups alike.

350g/12oz fresh raspberries or frozen raspberries slowly thawed
200g/7oz self raising flour
25g/1oz ground almonds
¼ tsp salt
½ tsp cinnamon
85g/3oz butter, softened
85g/3oz caster sugar
1 egg, beaten
150ml/¼ pint milk
1 tbsp raspberry jam
25g/1oz icing sugar
¼ pint double cream

Sift flour, almonds, salt and cinnamon into a bowl and rub in the butter, mix in the sugar. Add the beaten egg and milk to make a scone-like dough. Divide dough in two and gently shape each half to fit into greased 20cm/8in sandwich tins. Cook in a preheated oven at 230°C/450°F/Gas 8 for 10–15 minutes. Remove from the oven and cool on a wire rack. When cold spread one of the layers with raspberry jam, then generously with the double cream and raspberries. Sprinkle raspberries with icing sugar, cover with the second layer and top with more cream. Decorate with a few raspberries. Best eaten when fresh.

JP

Illustrated overleaf

Walnut and Marmalade Teabread

Marian MacNeill surmised that if every French woman was born with a saucepan in her hand every Scots woman was born with a rolling pin. I remember my Aberdonian grandmother saying she was referring to the Scottish ability to bake, not to deal with husbands when they came home drunk! Certainly when I was young it was the great test of a woman's suitability as a daughter-in-law. There is nothing nicer than the smell of baking through the house and it is one of my objections to microwaves that our children will grow up without the smell of food cooking. This is a very satisfying teabread for a lazy afternoon.

225g/8oz plain flour
pinch of salt
1 tbsp baking powder
115g/4oz butter
55g/2oz caster sugar
55g/2oz chopped walnuts
grated rind of 1 orange
2 eggs, beaten
3 tbsp marmalade
2–3 tbsp milk

Grease and carefully line a 450g/1lb loaf tin. Sift the flour, salt and baking powder into a bowl, rub in butter until the mixture resembles breadcrumbs. Stir in the sugar, nuts and rind. Add the eggs, the marmalade and sufficient milk to make a fairly soft batter. Turn into the loaf tin and bake in a preheated oven at 180°C/350°F/Gas 4 for 1¼–1½ hours or until well risen and golden brown. Turn out and cool on a wire rack.

CDW

Index